YELLOW WORKOUT BOOK: 52 BALANCE AND STRETCHING EXERCISES FOR SENIORS

TECHNIQUES AND EXERCISES FOR FALL PREVENTION, BETTER MOBILITY, STRENGTH, AND ENERGY. A GRADIENT APPROACH YOU CAN DO AT HOME

ROBERT L. STONEBRIDGE

Yellow
Workout Book

CONTENTS

INTRODUCTION

> "Do something today that your future self will thank you for."

— SEAN PATRICK FLANERY

The importance of taking care of your body and improving your standard of living is what this book is all about.

Things don't stay the same. They get better or worse. If you don't improve your physical strength and mobility on a regular basis, then chances are your strength and mobility will diminish. The way you want to live is up to you.

Every thirteen seconds an older person visits an emergency room because of damage caused by a fall. As you grow older, the consequences of your falls can become a lot more serious and even fatal. One bad fall can drastically impact your mobility.

If you're tired of the constant aches and pains that comes with old age. If you struggle to do the simple things that were once so easy for you. Then it's time to get into action and do something about it. It won't solve itself.

No one wants to find themselves unable to do things for themselves due to a fear of a fall and an injury, or just being a problem to the people in their lives. You don't want to have to rely on others because you still desire that independence.

Everything in life is done on a gradient, and no one ever climbed mount Everest in a day. Some say the first step toward any activity or journey is the most important. That may be true, but there are a lot of people in the world that only take that first step and never get to where they intended to go. The next step is the most important! That step that will take you to your destination and achieve your goals.

The exercises within this book will help you to conquer the physical issues you may be facing with older age. Robert is a rehab and strength-training instructor who has been helping seniors improve their quality of life for many decades. He knows what a huge difference it can make to even the simplest tasks and activities. His exercises and tips throughout this book will be exactly what you need to help your body strengthen, improve endurance and age gracefully.

The goal here is to be able to play with your grandchildren, have the stamina to practice activities that bring you joy, to feel independent and empowered, to have more energy, more mental clarity, and peace so that you may enjoy your years ahead with positivity and bliss.

There's a story of an elderly gentleman that spent 4 months going to the gym in the fall and winter of that year. He would show up every day to do exercises and lift weights. It didn't matter if it was raining or snowing outside, he still went to the gym daily. When Christmas time came around, he didn't show up. Then the new year came, and the older gentleman still didn't come back to the gym. The staff at the gym got concerned, so the owner decided to pay this gentleman a house visit to check up on him.

The older man answered his door with his 4-year-old grand-daughter in his arms. His family behind him in the living room. The gym owner asked if he was all right and let him know that he was missed back at the gym. The older gentleman smiled and assured the gym owned that he would definitely be coming back in the new week. He thanked the gym owner for his help and care. As the gym owner started down the front steps, the older gentleman called out his name. The gym owner turned around to see the older gentleman still standing in the doorway of his house. Smiling. With a twinkle in his eye the older gentleman said, "Thank you! Because you and your gym I can now do this." He then looked to his granddaughter who was still in his arms. Still smiling he walked inside his house with his granddaughter still in his arms.

Every activity has a goal. Take some time now to consider reasons why you want to improve your mobility and physical health. Maybe you want to be able to walk up and down the stairs at your house with ease, or you'd like to participate in some of your favorite activities that you haven't been able to participate in for years. This book will help you to achieve any of these goals you aspire to accomplish.

In this book you will learn easy-to-do home exercises that will drastically improve your overall physical health and happiness. You may even find that practicing in these exercises will boost your mental health as your strength, balance and mobility improve. From this book, you will become more resilient and learn how you can introduce activity into your lifestyle so that you find a routine that makes you healthier and stronger!

A wise man once told me that life was made to be lived. You are in it already so make the best of it.

Get to doing the things that bring you happiness.

1

WHY WE NEED BALANCE AND STRENGTH

"Birthdays are good for you. Statistics show that the people who have the most live the longest."

— LARRY LORENZONI

As the average person surpass the age of 65, falls can be a lot more damaging. It's the main cause of serious injury for most individuals in this age group.

A person in this age group should work toward improving their balance and strength so that falls doesn't become a challenge for them in the future. You want to work on yourself regularly so you can reduce the risk of harmful or fatal falls.

CONSEQUENCES OF FALLS

Approximately 36 million falls are reported to occur amongst the elderly every year, which sadly results in more than 32,000 deaths. Serious falls can cause' such thangs as head trauma, internal bleeding, bone fractures amongst other injuries. It can greatly reduce one's quality of life.

Nothing good can come out of any fall. The idea is to not get into that situation where a fall can happen. The best way to do that is to get or stay physically fit. With strength training, staying limber with stretches and sharpening one's senses, including one's sense of balance.

THE IMPORTANCE OF STRENGTH TRAINING AND BALANCE EXERCISES

As we grow older, we need to take the necessary precautions to prevent accidents from happening, by practicing both strength training and balance exercises!

You want to work on your strength and balance so that you can become less susceptible to falls, there are some effective strength training exercises and balance exercises that you should explore. Working on strength training and balancing together will help you to prevent falls, which ultimately decreases your risk of having serious injuries. Here are a few reasons why practicing in both activities will benefit you and reduce your risk of falling:

- **Effect on bone density.** Strength training promotes increased bone density. As you age, your bone density can decrease. Which makes one more fragile, as your bones are more brittle. The consequences are, if you fall with a lower bone density, you are more likely to experience serious injuries. By increasing one's bone density with strength training you greatly reduce your chances of fractures and brakes if a fall would take place.
- **Promotes weight loss.** One of the greatest benefits of practicing in these activities is that it promotes weight loss. Believe it or not but weight loss can help you be more stable and balanced. This is because you have more control over your body and a greater center of gravity, which will reduce your risk of falling easily.
- **Improving muscle mass and growth.** These types of activities will strengthen your muscles, which can result in muscle mass growth. The more you exercise, the more stamina you will have, which will help you to develop muscle and physical resilience. This will ultimately help you to become stronger and more stable. You will find that these exercises also keep your joints and bones healthy, which can relieve pain in your joints.
- **Healthy aging.** These exercises are important because they motivate healthy aging. The sooner you get started with these exercises, the better, as it will promote healthy and steady aging. You will experience less aches and pains that inhibit you from moving around, as well as you will be healthier and experience less detrimental

and terminal illnesses as you age. Not only will you age gracefully physically, but you will also age healthily mentally. You become less anxious, depressed, and your moods become more positive and stable.

- **Boosts your energy.** By embracing strength training and other forms of exercise you will feeling a boost in your energy levels. Being physically active can provide you with energy in the moment that you never knew you had. Although exercising may make you tired at first, by causing you to sleep more, after a long period of time you will see a massive boost in your energy levels.

There is nothing negative that comes from exploring safe exercises in your older age. Practicing both strength training and balancing exercises together will help you to get in such great shape that you feel like you're in your 40's again. This will drastically improve your quality of life.

HOW TO INTRODUCE YOURSELF TO STRENGTH TRAINING

Some people may feel intimidated by the term strength training because it sounds very physically intense. Others may struggle to walk properly or get up stairs. So, what is the bast way to practice strength training? Just like anything you learn or start doing, strength training is done on a gradient. One level at a time. When you feel you have that level and can do it easily you move up to the next level. Until that level is done with relative ease, and you go to the next level. Next thing you know you are feeling stronger, younger and happier as your mobility and activity increases.

Levels of Strength Training

It's important to realize that there are different levels of intensity when it comes to strength training. If you aren't that mobile then you can explore less intense levels of strength training, whereas, if you want to push yourself because you're still very mobile but you want to prevent your strength from deteriorating, then you can explore more intense training. This is how you can approach strength training:

- **Start at a lower level.** When you get started with your exercising journey, it's best to approach lower levels of strength training first. By starting at a lower level, it gives your body a chance to build and strengthen your tendons and supporting muscles so as to prevent straining or injuring yourself as you do strength training.
- **Level up when you're comfortable.** When the level you are on becomes easy to do and you no longer are sore the from the exercise then it is time to move up to the next level. You want to push yourself gradually so that you can become stronger over time. You shouldn't jump to intense exercises straight away, as you need to work yourself up to more intense exercises.
- **Be consistent.** To have success with exercise at any age, it is important to be consistent. If you want to see results, you need to exercise regularly. The more

consistent you are, the easier the exercises will become, and this will result in all the physical and mental benefits you've been desiring.

Before starting this journey, it's valuable for you to determine what level of fitness and mobility you're at. This will help you to realize what level of training to start with. You want to ensure that you start with what's in your comfort zone, so you enjoy it instead of getting hurt.

Setting Objectives

An activity without an objective can seem like a useless one. You have to have a place you want to arrive at. That's why it's important to have objectives that will keep you going. After you have an objective, you will need to create the habit or system to help you keep the course. Some common examples of objectives include the following:

- **Moving around is easier.** Some want to exercise so that they can move around easier. When people age, they may struggle to get from point A to point B as easily as they used to, even if the travel is from their room to the kitchen. This can make life extremely challenging because of aches and pains hold you back from moving around freely. Or they just want to be able to walk up and down the stairs with no issues.
- **Preventing the aging process.** Many are in good shape for their age. This may make them think they don't require exercise. However, exercising is valuable

because it can help prevent the effects of aging in your body. By getting active and exercising earlier in your life, rather than waiting until there is a problem you are trying to remedy the batter it will be for you. The idea is to age gracefully and feel youthful even when you approach your 80's.

- **Building confidence.** There are those that want to build confidence physically as well as mentally. As one gets older you may notice that there are bit of the body that get saggy or floppy. By regularly exercising, it will help tone and strengthen your body. And the more active and physically fit one gets, the more confident they'll feel in themselves. Many of the exercises in this book will help with these types of objectives.

Think to yourself what is the main problem that you're experiencing from aging that you want to eliminate through becoming stronger. It can be any of the options above, or your own unique reason. Once you discover what your objectives are to get fitter and stronger, it's important for you to write this down somewhere and look at it frequently. This will remind you and help motivate you toward a better standard of living.

Find an Exercise Partner

You may find that you enjoy strength training, and you experience the benefits, but you struggle to get yourself to stick to it. You are consistent for a few days a week, but after a while you find yourself wanting to give up. Finding an exercise partner is a great way for you to stay consistent and accountable. You can ask another of the same age group as you, a friend, your partner, or a family member to practice these exercises with you.

This will not only help you, but it will also benefit them physically and mentally. It also provides you with an opportunity for you to socialize, which can help you mentally. You're more likely to stick to your exercises program when you're doing it with someone who has the same interests.

REAL LIFE STORIES

Here are some stories of others that benefited from putting in an exercise program. These stories come from others that took action after a fall and injury and recovered. But ideally it doesn't take a serious accident to inspire one to do something about their physical condition. Ideally one would progress and maintain their physical condition through exercise and nutrition so they are not the effect of a bad accident or fall.

Annie's Story

When we think of falling, we assume it will happen in a dangerous environment with uneven ground or hazardous objects in the way. However, bad falls can even occur in the comfort of your own home. One can avoid going outside to prevent falls, but it can happen easily anywhere. Annie's story is a great testament to this.

Annie experienced one bad fall when she was on a walk, as she tripped on the curb, and this left her in a boot for a while during recovery. However, most of her falls occurred in her house, especially in her bathroom. Annie said that these falls didn't happen because she tripped or slipped, but they occurred due to her dizziness from being ill. These instances where she had fallen, she called the paramedics for help because she was unable to get up on her own.

She realized that this way of living in fear and pain was not for her anymore, so she transformed her life with exercise. She entered a fall prevention program which helped her to live a better quality of life.

John's Story

Sometimes all it takes is one bad fall to impact you negatively. For John, it was one fall that ultimately changed his life and quality of life. He experienced a fall that injured his back severely. A disk in his back that got damaged and effected the functioning of his left leg. This left him struggling to walk around, which drastically impacted his mobility.

From that moment, his wife enrolled him into fall prevention classes, to prevent something like this from ever occurring again. Through these classes, he realized the most important thing to prevent falls is not to stop walking and moving around. Walking became extremely necessary for his recovery and strength. He had to be mindful of his path ahead of him as he walked and exercised. And in so doing, he became more aware of obstacles and his environment around him. This has also helped him prevent further falls as he sees the consequences of the path he takes.

2

AS WE GET OLDER

"*Inaction breeds doubt and fear. Action breeds confidence and courage. If you want to conquer fear, do not sit home and think about it. Go out and get busy.*"

— DALE CARNEGIE

Getting older is inevitable for all of us. Each birthday brings with it another year lived. One can look at this and feel bad that they aren't as youthful as they once were and sit there feeling sorry for themselves or feel it's not worth doing something about their physical condition. Or you can get up and take that next step towards a more youthful feeling life. Life is here to enjoy. As in your youth, the sky is still blue, and the sun is still worm. The beauty of the world is all around you. From the fragrant flowers to the green on a golf course. Take advantage of the time you have ahead of you and not dwell on the past. There is as much life in the world as you inject into it. And that is all the life there will ever be, so if you haven't already, take Mr. Carnegie's advice and get into action and go out and get busy!

HOW YOUR BODY AGES

Just like it takes time for one's body to degrade to where it is hard to move around and painful, it also takes time to build the body back up. But the good news is, is that you can build the body back up! It does take work, but it is extremely gratifying. Just imagine getting out and doing the things you loved to do when you were younger. Let it be hitting the green or playing pickleball. Whatever it is these activities can be done again.

And if you are already living life and enjoying it, just remember, aging is a gradual process, and with the proper stretches, exercise and nutrition these activities can be enjoyed longer.

Stretching, exercise and nutrition are so important toward preventative aging. Once you're starting to age and you're only noticing small signs of it, it's important to work toward slowing down this process. You want to be mobile, strong, and youthful for as long as possible.

Causes of Aging

You may find that some people age more gracefully, whereas there are other people who look even older than they actually are. The causes of age vary, and some of the reasons are either uncontrollable or they're in your control. You can't prevent yourself from aging altogether. However, you can work toward aging more gradually and gracefully so that you can make the most of the rest of your life! These are some circumstances and behavior that can cause rapid aging:

- **Stress.** If you've lived a long life of stress every day, it's going to take a massive toll on your body as you age. When we stress, we don't realize the negative impact it has on our physical health. Did you have or still have an extremely stressful and demanding job? If you put yourself under strenuous circumstances that cause intense stress frequently, it will catch up with you as you start to age.
- **Genes.** Of course, one of the uncontrollable factors of aging that you can't really influence are your genes. You can't control the genes you have, so it's important to look at the people in your family from generations before you, to determine if it's common in your family to age rapidly. Although this may be in your genes, you can do activities and work to counteract it. This just means that you may have to put in a little extra work.
- **Unhealthy habits.** Another cause of rapid aging are unhealthy daily habits. The behavior and actions you choose to do when you're younger, can have a massive influence on how you age. If you didn't look after your body when you were younger, it will most probably reflect negatively in your later years. For example, if you smoked every day, consumed a lot of alcohol,

avoided exercise, and had an unhealthy diet, it will have a negative impact on your health as you age.

Unfortunately, we can't undo the things we may have done in the past that will catch up with us in our old age, but fortunately, what we can do is ensure that we work on ourselves now while we still can. It's never too late to work on your health because you have the power to turn around your negative circumstances and aging side effects.

Signs Your Body Is Aging

You may have already noticed that your body isn't as strong or resilient as it used to be, you get tired more easily, and you don't look as youthful anymore. However, sometimes it can be challenging to notice aging signs, as we age gradually without seeing drastic change. You want to be able to observe the signs of your body aging so that you can work on regaining your strength and youthfulness.

Remember that your age shouldn't limit your mobility, activity capability, and your self-confidence. You can defy your aging process by doing the right exercises that build your strength and resilience. Let's first discuss the physical signs of aging you may notice first:

- **Decreased muscle mass.** One of the physical signs you may notice when you're aging is that you have a massive decrease in your muscle mass. If you have great muscles in your arms and torso, you may notice that they have shrunk in size and your skin is more loose, and with fatty tissue.

- **Wrinkles.** The most feared sign of aging for most people are wrinkles. You may look in the mirror and notice crow's feet, frown lines, and wrinkles on your neck—which makes you think it's the end of the world, you're getting old! You shouldn't define your youthfulness by the amount of wrinkles on your face and body, even though they are a sign that your body is aging.

- **Healing slower.** Another physical sign that you're aging is when your injuries take longer to heal. When you're younger and you hurt yourself, your body works like a well-oiled machine to heal it. As you age, your body finds it more challenging to heal your cuts, bruises, and fractures. You may find that a simple bruise takes forever to heal.

It's important for you to realize that looks aren't everything when it comes to aging. Yes, you may have a few wrinkles and your body doesn't look as great as it used to, but the true testament of health and youthfulness can be seen through your physical wellbeing. These are some more subtle signs of aging that you may feel and sense:

- **Overly fatigued.** We all experience fatigue—because let's face it—life can be pretty draining. However, if you find yourself feeling overly fatigued frequently, it's an indicator that you're growing older. You don't have the energy to do the activities you used to enjoy, you nap during the day. And even after sleeping you still feel tired, which can be extremely frustrating.

- **Aches and pains.** Do you notice aches and pains when you do simple things such as walking? If your body, muscles, and joints experience pain easily, it's a sign of physical aging. Your body becomes weaker, which causes any source of activity to have a toll on your body. This is why it's important to exercise, to make yourself stronger and less susceptible to these aches and pains.

- **Mental deterioration.** Another way to notice whether you're aging or not is by taking a look at your mental state. Do you forget things more easily, or do you struggle to think of answers and solutions as easily? If your mental state is deteriorating along with your physical body, you need to work on strengthening yourself holistically. We can focus so much on our physical body aging, that we neglect the wellbeing of our mind, which will be discussed in more detail further along in this chapter.

Aging Internally

Now that you're able to establish how you're aging by the way you feel and look, it's important to know what happens internally as you grow older. Unfortunately, as you age your body starts to function less effectively, which can negatively impact your health holistically. These are some common internal effects of aging:

- **Resorption.** At the age of 50, your body starts the process of resorption, which means your bones breakdown. This is why your bones become more fragile and delicate. This is what makes falling down so frightening for seniors, because it may not result in a few bruises. A fall can cause fractures and bone damage that can be extremely detrimental to your mobility.
- **Vascular system changes.** Your blood vessels don't function the way they used to. You may find that you're struggling with high blood pressure, which could have a multitude of negative impacts on your overall health. Although it may not have many side effects, it can result in some fatal ones if left untreated. You could experience a stroke or heart attack, both of which can be fatal.
- **Eyesight.** A very common aging side effect that you may experience is deteriorated eyesight. You may have had perfect eyesight in your earlier adulthood years, without even wearing glasses, but now that you're getting older, the lenses of your eyes become less flexible. This means you struggle to see objects up close, which is known as presbyopia. Experiencing this decrease in eyesight can ultimately result in you tripping and falling, because you misjudge the perspective of objects around you.

Aging externally is hard enough, you don't look or feel the way you used to. Aging internally can be even scarier because it can drastically impact your health. Some of these health issues you may experience from old age can actually be life threatening. Being able to work on yourself through exercise will not only help you to move around with more ease, but it can also reduce your risk of experiencing dangerous and fatal health issues.

MIND AND BODY CONNECTION

When we consider the aging of your body as you get older, it's also valuable to keep your mind in consideration. Your mind and body are connected, so if your body starts to deteriorate, you will find that your mental state follows. Aging can be challenging for us mentally for a number of reasons, so it's important to do what you can to lessen this negative side effect.

Although exercise may seem like it's focused on your physical health, it can actually have a drastic positive impact on your mind as well. When you're active and physically strong, it can not only stimulate your brain to function efficiently, but it also helps you to feel better mentally about yourself and this phase of your life. These are some of the ways aging can have a negative impact on your mental state.

Depression

Getting old can be depressing for many people. This state of depression can get worse when you experience physical signs of aging, especially when they prevent you from living life the way you're used to. Some causes of depression in seniors include the following:

- **Low concentration of folate in blood.** One of the reasons why you may be struggling with depression in old age is because of the contents of your blood. This means that there's a lack of Vitamin B in your blood, which helps you make red blood cells. This lack of red blood cells in your blood could lead to anemia.
- **Not being able to live freely.** It can be a challenging concept to grasp mentally knowing that you're going from a busy and independent life, to a lifestyle where you have to depend on others. You can't do all the activities that have normally brought you happiness, because your physical state holds you back. You may be perfect mentally, but physically you feel your age. This can be extremely frustrating because you don't want to let go of the life you love, and guess what? You don't have to! With the right exercises you can enjoy your life safely.
- **Social isolation.** Another prominent issue amongst seniors that causes depression is experiencing social isolation. As you get older you may find that you have less and less people in your life. You may not have the social life you used to have.

Exercising can get you out of this depressive state of mind. However, exercise won't only help you to conquer your physical aging issues, but it can also provide you with the opportunity to socialize with others! When you exercise, you can meet

other people, depending on the exercises you want to participate in. We'll go into detail on how you can meet people later
on in the book.

Dementia

Another way you may experience mental effects from aging is
through your memory. It's very common for individuals as they
age to have a decrease in their memory. Experiencing dementia
can be extremely frustrating because your mental state declines
dramatically, without you having a sense of control. These are
some signs and side effects of dementia:

- **Memory loss.** One of the main, most common signs of
  dementia, is memory loss. If you're starting to struggle
  to remember things both short-term and long-term, it's
  a sign of mental decline. You can forget things from
  your past that make you who you are, or you may forget
  things that have happened ten minutes ago. You can
  even forget who you are and what you were trying to
  say mid-sentence.
- **Difficulty communication.** Another sign of dementia
  that you may experience is the inability to
  communicate and articulate yourself properly. Your
  grasp of words isn't the same as it used to be. You may
  know what you're feeling but you don't know how to
  translate that into words. This is frustrating because
  you can't get other people to understand you.
- **Confusion and disorientation.** If you're in the more
  severe stages of dementia, you will find that you feel

disoriented and confused. You forget why you're where you are, and you can even feel lost in locations that you know. Your sense of direction gets lost because you forget how roads and areas look. When you get confused and disorientated, you need to have a family member or caretaker around so that you don't find yourself lost and in trouble.

- **Depression and paranoia.** Dementia doesn't only impact you mentally and physically, but it can also have a psychological effect on you. When you experience memory loss, difficulty communicating, and confusion, it can put you in a very dark space. You don't feel like yourself which can make you extremely depressed. It can also make you really paranoid, as you always feel like something is going to go wrong or that other people are against you.

Although dementia is often caused by old age and genetics, it can be prevented or treated with the proper diet and exercise. By keeping your body active and healthy it improves the strength of your mental state. Other things that can help you to prevent dementia is keeping an active mind, keeping your body moving physically, getting sufficient sleep, and maintaining a social life.

Other Mental Health Issues

There are other mental health issues that are common amongst seniors. Unfortunately, it's common for the mental health of older people to deteriorate, as they aren't constantly stimulated, as well as their physical health declines.

- **Anxiety.** You may think that old age comes with peace and serenity because you don't have the stress of work and overwhelming responsibilities. Although this may be the case for many seniors, lots of individuals of older age experience quite the opposite. They start to feel out of control, which makes them extremely anxious. You may find that you have a heightened level of stress and anxiety in your older age, as you worry for your future, your family, and the people around you.
- **Personality disorders.** If you experienced personality disorders such as paranoia, OCD, narcissism, and schizoid when you're younger, there's a big chance that these disorders will worsen as you get older. You may have not gotten any symptoms for these disorders in decades, but you may find that they sneak up on you in your later years.
- **Substance abuse.** Many seniors who feel depressed and anxious abuse substances to relieve them of their mental and emotional pain. Some seniors have addictive habits such as drinking, gambling, and smoking, which only further hurts their physical and mental health. It's also common for seniors to overly indulge in pain killers, not just for the feeling it gives them but also to relieve them from aches and pain. Although this may relieve pain at the moment, it's not a sustainable solution.

If you identify with any of these mental health issues, disorders, and impairments, don't despair. You can work toward eliminating these negative thoughts and feelings you experience on a daily basis by exercising regularly. Being active and healthy will not only help you physically, but it will clear your mind mentally. It will fill you with confidence, clarity, and purpose, which will help you to have a more positive and resilient state of mind.

3

WHAT IS YOUR REAL RISK FACTOR?

"Risk comes from not knowing what you're doing."

— WARREN BUFFETT

L et's take a look at the facts. It's valuable to consider what your real risk factor is when it comes to experiencing falls that have harmful consequences. Calculating how at risk you are can help you to take the right measures to prevent yourself from falling in the future. This chapter will show you some ways you may be at risk, which may shock you.

WHAT CONTRIBUTES TO YOUR RISK OF FALLING

Before you consider anything, you need to have a better idea of what increases your risk of falling. We've already discussed some of the factors that would increase your risk of falling, but have you properly considered which factors you are at risk with? Let's go through a quick recap of the factors that contribute to your risk of falling.

- Decreased muscle strength which means you have a lack of balance and mobility.
- Impaired senses, hearing or vision, which can make you miss objects and people moving around you, causing you to fall.
- Being on medication that causes dizziness and other side effects that can increase your risk of falling.
- A hazardous home environment with slippery floors and objects in the way which can increase the risk of you falling.

Once you've gone through this list, you can consider whether you identify with any of these factors. If you do, it's valuable to keep these factors in mind as you move on to the next part of this chapter, figuring out how to assess your risk factor.

HOW TO ASSESS YOUR RISK OF FALLING

Now that you know what the contributors to falling are, you should ask yourself how you can assess your risk of falling. You can assess your risk of falling all by yourself, just by considering some of the factors that may make you more at risk than others. These are some questions you should answer when you're assessing your risk of falling:

- *What is your history of falling?* The first thing you should ask yourself is what is your fall history like. You can determine how much of a risk you are when you consider your history of falling. If you've never experienced a fall in your older age then you are at a low risk of falling in the future. If you have fallen a couple times but experienced no real or detrimental injuries, that means you're at a medium risk of falling and hurting yourself. However, if you've fallen in your older age and it has impacted your mobility then you're at higher risk.

- *What is your mental status?* Ask yourself whether your aging has impacted your mental health. Have you been struggling with memory loss, feeling disorientated, and experiencing intense depression or anxiety? If so, you're at a higher risk of falling as a senior. You may find yourself wandering off, getting lost, and falling because you're unaware of your surroundings.

- *Are you on medication, and if you are, what medication are you on?* The medication you take could have a huge impact on how much of a risk you are for falling. Unfortunately, as you get older your overall health decreases, which means your doctor may prescribe medication so that you can experience a better quality of life as a senior. If you're taking medication, you should take a look at the side effects that may be impacting your fall risk.

- *How good is your mobility?* One of the most important things to consider is how good your mobility is. If your mobility hasn't really changed in your older age, then your risk of falling as a senior decreases drastically. But, if your mobility is impaired, you struggle to walk up and down stairs, you need a walker to help you get around, and small walks are painful and challenging for you, your risk of falling will increase dramatically.

- *Do you have orthostatic hypotension?* Orthostatic hypotension is a form of low blood pressure, which can increase your risk of falling. It can cause dizziness and a light head, which can cause you to fall easily. When you stand up quickly you may feel unbalanced, like your body is going to topple over. You may even experience bouts of dizziness as you're walking normally, which can make you more prone to falling.

After answering these questions, what would you say your risk of falling is? Consider the answer to each one of these questions so that you can come to a fair and honest conclusion. The more of these questions you've given high risk answers to, the more likely you are to fall and hurt yourself.

HOW TO DECREASE YOUR FALL RISK

If you've just discovered that your fall risk is extremely high, this may leave you alarmed. You may find that you're fearful of moving around now because you don't want to experience a bad fall that could potentially lead you to your demise. It's important to realize that although having a high risk of failure is scary, it's not impossible to decrease.

Knowing exactly why you're falling can help you to target the issue by its root. This book will teach you how you can decrease your fall risk through being more physically active.

Believe it or not but practicing these exercises can actually help you solve all the issues that are making you a fall risk. These fitness tips will help you to tackle your risk of falling:

- **Know your limits.** First and foremost, you need to be aware of your limits when you're pursuing exercising. Your physical activity journey should be enjoyable and rewarding, not hurtful and risky. The point of this exercise is to become strong so that you don't have to worry about hurting yourself in the future. You need to identify when you're feeling dizzy and if you're about to fall or black out. You need to be able to stop exercising when your body is giving you signs that it shouldn't do anymore.
- **Check with a professional.** If you have aches and pains in your bones, ligaments, and muscles it's advisable for you to get a medical assessment before pursuing this exercise journey. A doctor will know how far you can push yourself without hurting yourself, as they are able to assess your body's limits.
- **Stay consistent.** You won't be able to decrease your fall risk if you aren't consistent with your exercises. When you're consistent, you will be able to do more exercises as your resilience increases. The more you do, the more you reduce your risk of falling. Being inconsistent with your exercises will not only stunt your growth and success in this process, but it will also make you more fatigued. We want a gradual increase in strength and balance and the only way to accomplish this is with consistency.

Your goal should be to eliminate every issue that you experience from the list above. You want to ensure that your mental status is great so that you don't find yourself in tricky situations. You may also want to look after your health so that you can get off medication that's putting you at risk, improve your mobility, and decrease any health risks that cause you to lose balance and fall.

FALL RISK ASSESSMENT

After reading this chapter, you still may be unaware of your risk factor when it comes to falling. You don't know how to determine what makes you more of a risk or not. This makes it valuable for you to take a fall risk assessment. You may not be fully considering all of the various elements that make you more of a fall risk. This simple, yet effective assessment will help you to have an accurate understanding of what your fall risk is.

To participate in an effective online assessment you can try out this one from finding balance which is completely free! You must answer a couple of questions which help to determine how much of a fall risk you are. If you'd like a second more accurate idea of your fall risk, you can go visit a doctor to find out.

4

OVERCOMING FALLING FEARS

> *"Fear keeps us focused on the past or worried about the future. If we can acknowledge our fear, we can realize that right now we are okay. Right now, today, we are still alive, and our bodies are working marvelously. Our eyes can still see the beautiful sky. Our ears can still hear the voices of our loved ones."*
>
> — THICH NHAT HANH

Although it's important to be aware of the risks that come with falling, it's important to not let this fear consume you. If you're constantly worried about falling, you will find that it comes in the way of your quality of life. You avoid doing things you enjoy because you're scared that you'll experience a hurtful fall that will impact you in the long-term.

WHY YOU'RE SCARED OF FALLING

After everything we've discussed in the previous chapters, you may be thinking to yourself that it's impossible for you to not be scared of falling. You now know the serious consequences of falling and how dangerous it can truly be, which can cause you to fear it immensely. You don't want to experience a fall that could ultimately be fatal for you.

It's completely understandable to be fearful of falling, especially if you've experienced a bad fall before. You've had a bad fall in your older age and it took ages for you to recover. It may have even negatively impacted your mobility, making it a struggle for you to walk and move around on a daily basis.

Experiencing a bad fall like this can be a traumatic experience. You don't have the balance and strength you used to have, so what will stop this from happening again in the future?

Approximately 20 to 60 percent of seniors have the fear of falling, and this causes them to limit the activities that they do throughout the day. If you're part of this percentage, then you may prevent yourself from doing the activities you love doing. You're less active, and things such as shopping and bathing can be a scary and painful experience for you.

This fear can be very overwhelming and it can drastically impact your quality of life. You don't want to let this fear stop you from living your life. This is why it's crucial for you to conquer this anxiety so that it doesn't stunt your happiness.

HOW TO OVERCOME YOUR FEAR

It's normal to be fearful of falling, but you can't let the fear consume you. It is crucial for you to be cautious and preventative, but you can't live your life fearing your every move because you don't want to fall. You need to be able to conquer this mental block that decreases your quality of life.

Identify Why You're Falling

If you've experienced a bad fall before and you find yourself out of balance countless times, you need to be able to identify why you're falling first. You can't conquer your fear and your issue if you don't know what's causing it. Take a look at this list of reasons for falling and consider which one suits your circumstances the most:

- **Poor balance.** If your body is unfit, you may struggle to balance, which makes you topple over and fall easily.
- **Impaired vision.** If your eyesight is bad, you may not be able to see things obstructing your path which can cause you to trip and fall.
- **Chronic diseases.** If you have diseases that cause your physical state to deteriorate then you could fall easier.
- **Lack of fitness.** If you're struggling with your fitness as a senior, it can make you more of a victim of falling. Simple activities can turn into hazards.

Once you determine what the cause of your falling is, you can now take the proper measures to work toward solving them.

For example, if you're falling because of your impaired vision, you can visit the optometrist and get a stronger prescription for your glasses. This will help you to see better, which will make you less likely to trip and fall. Conquering this issue will make you less anxious because you're solving the problem from its root.

Have a Plan

One of the scariest thoughts of falling is being stuck alone with no one to help you. Nobody likes to have a fear that they will be in a vulnerable and dangerous position all on their own. This is why it's valuable for you to make a plan for if you fall. Here is how you can prepare yourself for worst case scenario if you have a fall:

- **Have loved ones on speed dial.** If you find yourself experiencing a fall, it's valuable to have friends or family on speed dial. You can call them in an emergency so that they can help you. Give trusted ones the key to your home so that they can let themselves in when you're unable to get up. For this plan to work, you need to carry your phone around with you. If you were to fall, you need your phone on you so that you can quickly call your loved ones to help. It is also wise to have a smart phone. Like an Apple phone. You can use your voice and tell your phone to call someone for help.
- **Fall proof your house.** Another way you can go about planning ahead is by preventing any fall threats in your home. You can ensure that falling hazards in your house

are eliminated, so it's something you don't have to worry about so much. For example, if you have tile stairs that are slippery, you can install a carpet; or if you struggle to get up the stairs you can add a railing to support you. By fall proofing your house you can be less anxious of falling.

- **Get a caretaker.** If you're really worried and you feel as though you don't have the strength or energy to look after yourself, it may be a good idea to look into getting a caretaker. The sound of this may be depressing, but if you get started with your exercises but you still feel vulnerable and fearful, having a caretaker to look after you will provide you with a remarkable peace of mind.

Stay Active

The best way for you to conquer your fear of falling is by staying active. One of the most common reasons why you may fall is because your body has lost strength and balance. Even if your past falls were caused by something, chances are you'd be able to save yourself from falling or you wouldn't have injured yourself severely if your body was stronger and fitter.

Throughout this book you're going to learn how to stay active as a senior. You will soon learn the specific exercises that can help prevent falls. Once you become stronger and more balanced, you will feel more prepared if you find yourself in a falling position. Not only will you be able to catch yourself but if you do fall it won't be as harmful as it could have been.

Challenge Your Negative Thoughts

If you're overwhelmed by fear when it comes to falling and exercising, you need to challenge these thoughts. You don't want to end up being your own worst enemy who holds yourself back in life. Instead of dwelling in your thoughts and letting it stop you from living your life, you must eliminate these negative thoughts. These are some ways you can successfully challenge your thoughts:

- **Build confidence.** When you find yourself feeling self-conscious and scared about your safety, you need to instill confidence within yourself. You need to learn how to trust yourself and your ability to prevent falls. As soon as you sense the negative thoughts, reassure yourself that you are doing what is necessary to prevent yourself from getting injured. You will find that being active and exercising regularly will instill the self-confidence you need that will eliminate negative thoughts.
- **Look at the positive side.** Another way for you to challenge any negative thoughts is by transforming these unhelpful thoughts into positive and encouraging ones. Instead of dwelling on the possibility of you being hurt, you can think about how hard you'll work to protect yourself. Knowing that you're working hard can give you a more positive and refreshing perspective that assures you this won't be an issue for.

It's all about your own perspective and mental state. You can choose to have a fearful and anxious approach to falling, or you can empower and encourage yourself to terminate all threats of falling. You're going to feel negative if you don't work toward changing your circumstances. However, if you make the necessary changes then you can have a more positive perspective because you know you're strong enough to eliminate this fear.

Talk to Someone About Your Fears

If you feel as though your fears and concerns about falling are truly overwhelming, it's valuable to reach out to people that care about you. It's not a silly or irrational fear that you have to keep to yourself, because people will understand why it scares you and can help. Sometimes talking about it and getting a different perspective on the issue will help to manage your anxiety.

It's also valuable for you to gather a support group of people in a similar age group as you. Maybe you can reach out to old friends, talk to people around the same age as you, and even find online support groups for seniors. Talking to people with the same fears as you can help you to feel less anxious toward the idea of falling.

HOW TO ELIMINATE YOUR FEAR OF EXERCISE

If you find yourself really stressed and fearful of falling and injuring yourself, this may prevent you from pursuing exercise. In order to prevent yourself from falling and hurting yourself, you need to practice the necessary exercises, so you need to eliminate your fear of doing physical activities. Once you get rid of your fear of exercise, you'll be able to get stronger which will make you less fearful of falling or getting an injury. Here are some ways you can eliminate your fear of exercise.

Do Your Stretches

To prepare your body for exercise, it's important for you to do your stretches beforehand. It gets your muscles, ligaments, and entire body ready to be exercised. Doing this will prevent any injuries, which can make you feel more at ease to workout. You should practice these stretches before and after your workout so that you don't wear and tear on your body.

Warm Ups

Warm ups are the stretches and worm up exercises that you do before you start your actual exercises. This helps to prepare your body for the activity you're about to do. Your body may be rusty, especially if you haven't done proper exercises in a long time. It's crucial for you to do warm ups because you don't want to end up pulling something or hurting yourself. These are some suitable examples of warm ups for seniors:

- **Dynamic stretches.** The best way for you to warm up your body is by doing dynamic stretches. These are controlled muscle movements that introduce your body to different movements. We will explore various dynamic stretches in more depth further along in the book. Some examples of dynamic stretches include leg circles, ankle roll, shoulder roll, and arm circles.

- **Seated exercises.** Because seated exercises are so low-intensive, most of them can be used as a warm up for your body. These exercises are practiced slowly, and their main purpose is to stretch out your muscles and worm them up. In the next chapter, you will discover all of the seated exercises that you can use as a warm up for your muscles.

- **Walking.** If you aren't the stretching type of person and you don't want to do stretches both before and after your exercise, then walking is a great way to warm up those muscles. It gets your blood flowing and warms up your body in the same way dynamic stretches do. You can also try other forms of cardio like cycling to warm up those muscles.

When it comes to warming up, it's important for you to warm up the parts of your body that you're going to be exercising. If you are going to have a day where you focus on your legs, your upper body, or your core, you must ensure that you do stretching that introduces movement to these muscles.

Cool Downs

Cool downs are exercises you must do after your exercises. These stretches help to prevent pain the next day. If you're rusty with fitness, then one day of exercise can leave you stiff and filled with pain the next day. Doing cool downs will prevent this from happening, as well as it will prepare the next day to do more exercises. Here are some cool downs you can practice after your exercises:

- **Simple stretches.** You are probably exhausted after your exercises, as you pushed yourself to your limits. This means that you can't even imagine yourself doing some strenuous stretches. You can try out some simple and easy stretches that we will explore in more detail shortly. Some examples of simple stretches for your cool down include chin to chest stretch, tricep stretch, and ear to shoulder stretch. There are many more that we will cover in this book. But the idea is to move the body.
- **Yoga.** One of the best ways for you to cool down after a productive workout is by doing some yoga. There are various yoga poses that allow you to stretch out your muscles such as the pigeon pose, child pose, and tree pose. Practicing yoga will help you wind down physically.
- **Walking.** This is a great way to cool down after a workout. Walking for several minutes can greatly reduce sourness the next day.

Doing stretches will be discussed in more depth further along in the book. We can often forget how important stretching is for our health because we focus on the exercises, but stretching makes your physical activity more effective. Stretching will also improve your balance and strength which can prevent falls.

Breathing exercises

Now you're ready to exercise so that you can strengthen both your body and mind, but the thought of starting can makes you anxious. Thinking like this can be very overwhelming because you're stuck in a negative loop. You want to exercise to prevent yourself from hurting yourself, but you don't want to hurt yourself by exercising.

Thinking like this will prevent you from ever exercising because you're constantly overwhelmed by your anxiety. This makes it valuable for you to practice some breathing exercises before you exercise so you can get yourself calm and centered. It will also help you to center your body, which will make you have a greater sense of control over yourself physically as you practice exercises. This is how you can go about practicing a breathing exercise before your workout:

1. **Breathe in.** Start off in a comfortable position, whether you're lying down, sitting, or standing up, ensure you're comfortable. You must then breathe in to the count of three and as you breathe in, relax all of the muscles in your body.
2. **Breathe out.** After you've held your breath in for a few seconds, you can then breathe out to the count of three. As you exhale slowly, you must focus on each part of your body. Ensure that each part of your body releases any tension so that you're even more relaxed physically.
3. **Repeat.** You can then repeat this process again and again until you feel a sense of calm. Ensure that you're

counting your inhales and exhales so that you're controlling your breathing effectively. As you breathe, you should breathe through your nose so that the air enters your belly, and you can breathe out through your mouth.

There are various breathing activities out there that you can try. We often forget how powerful deep breathing can be, especially when we're feeling anxious. Starting your exercises off with breathing activities will help you to have a relaxed body, which will make your exercise more productive.

When you practice strength training it may feel natural for you to hold your breath, but you need to continue using your deep breathing as you lift weights or practice any form of exercise because it will allow you to be in control.

Get Comfortable

Exercising for the first time after a while can be a stressful experience. You don't know where to start and you don't know if you're doing exercises right. The last thing you want to worry about is what you're wearing and the equipment you're using. You may be thinking to yourself that you don't have the high end workout clothing and equipment that will help you, but at the end of the day the most important aspect of your clothing should be comfort!

You want to be comfortable throughout your exercise, so it's important to ensure that the following aspects of your workout are taken care of suitably:

- **Wear comfortable clothes.** The clothes that you wear during an exercise is important because if you wear the wrong clothing it can restrict you from moving effectively. You want to wear loose fitting clothes that give you breathing room and make you feel comfortable. When you're exercising the last thing you want to be focused on is pulling up your pants or not being able to do a movement because your clothes are hugging you tight.

- **Use the right shoes.** Depending on what level of exercises you're exploring, the type of shoes you wear is important. If you're practicing seated or lying down exercises, your shoes aren't as important. However, if you are doing standing up and moving exercises, you want to ensure your shoes are comfortable. Get your most comfortable shoes that you're able to walk and move around in without getting blisters or feet pain. You can even forego shoes to work out barefoot if that makes you more comfortable.

- **Use safe equipment.** Your clothing isn't the only thing you should consider when you're trying to have a comfortable exercising experience. You should also take time to look at the equipment you're using to exercise with. It needs to be safe and usable so that you don't end up hurting yourself. For example, if you're using a chair for exercises, you want to ensure that it's stable and won't move or break when you use it.

Start Gradually

When starting to exercise it is important to start and progress on a gradient. All things progress or digress on a gradient. Nothing stays the same forever.

Here are three aspects of an exercise that you should intensify gradually:

- **Tempo.** The first thing you should consider is how fast you're doing the exercises. When you're starting off, you must exercise at a slow and steady rate. You need to pace yourself because you're not going to have the stamina you may have had when you're younger. There's nothing wrong with doing them slowly and steadily, as long as you're controlling your muscles and making the most of each exercise.
- **Quantity.** You also need to consider the quantity of exercises that you practice. When you're planning your exercises, you need to be realistic with your expectations. Remember that it's your first time exercising in a while, so you need to take it easy and not overdo it. Being realistic when planning your exercises prevents you from injuring yourself by pushing past your current limits. If your body is starting to feel weak, you feel dizzy, light headed, or nauseous then call it a day for your exercise.
- **Resistance and intensity.** Starting off with exercise means that you should introduce yourself to a lower

intensity of exercise. When you're practicing strength training, you want to start off by lifting lighter weights. Try out the simpler and less intense exercises before you explore the exercises that will make you break a sweat. Once you warm up with lower intense and resistant exercises, you want to work your way up to higher intensities so that you're challenging your body and strengthening it in the process.

With any exercise that you do, you must start off at a level that is manageable. You want the exercise to be enjoyable for you, so you want to push yourself in an appropriate manner without going too over the top. The most important thing is to practice consistency because this is when you'll see growth. The more you practice slow, low-intensity exercises, the easier it will be for you to level up the intensity.

PREPARATION EXERCISE

Sometimes we need to mentally prepare ourselves to do something that is out of our comfort zone. Once you mentally prepare yourself to be more active, it will make you comfortable and capable of practicing all the exercises coming up in this book.

When you want to practice preparation successfully, you need to be able to change your mindset, especially if you find yourself having a negative attitude toward exercising. Doing a preparation exercise will help you to look at yourself in a new light, where you know you're capable of fulfilling all these beneficial exercises. Follow these steps to prepare yourself for the exercises you want to accomplish:

1. **Clear negative thoughts.** The first thing you want to do when practicing this activity is to clear your mind of all negative thoughts making you doubt yourself. If you doubt that you can exercise, you're not going to be able to envision yourself doing it. Have an unbiased mindset where you don't think about how unfit you might be or how much you dislike exercise.

2. **Visualize yourself in gear.** To start off this exercise, you can get yourself prepared with your exercise gear. Consider what exercise clothing you'll be wearing. You can go into your closet and choose an exercise outfit that would be most suitable for your workout session. You should then put on this exercise gear and go to the place where you'd like to exercise. Ensure that you're prepared with everything you may need like a water bottle, chair, or matt. This will get you prepared and into the mindset of starting your exercise.

3. **Read through each exercise.** To ensure that you're doing these exercises properly, you need to read through each exercise in this book thoroughly. Instead of just jumping into each exercise, you must prepare yourself by understanding how you must perform each movement. Once you're familiar with your exercises after reading through them, you're ready to get started!

You may want to do this preparation for seated exercises, because that's what is coming up in the next chapter. Before you start the exercises that follow, you can use these steps to get you into the right mental space. This will make you feel more prepared to accomplish the exercises that follow.

5

SEATED EXERCISES

> "Your health account, your bank account, they're the same thing. The more you put in, the more you can take out."
>
> — JACK LALANNE

If your mobility isn't at its best and you're fearful of just jumping into exercises, this is the best place for you to start. You should start with low impact seated exercises that will go easy on your body. We will explore various safe seated exercises, as well as lying exercises.

STARTING OFF YOUR JOURNEY

You're starting off your exercising journey and if you're feeling a bit anxious because you don't know where and how to begin. This is a guide for you We're beginning with an easy, safe, and manageable starting point for any senior to try. We are going to start off by discussing some seated exercises that you can use to introduce your body to exercise.

Benefits of Starting Off With Seated Exercises

Seated exercises are a good form of exercise that can safely integrate exercise into your everyday life. With these you need to start off light, especially if you struggle with your mobility and your overall health. These are some benefits you can experience by starting with seated exercises:

- **You'll feel comfortable.** One of the main reasons why seated exercises are so beneficial is because they help you to feel comfortable starting off this journey. It's a great and safe way for you to introduce yourself to exercise, as it's not strenuous and demanding of your physical strength. You will find that you're more willing to fully embrace these exercises because you know that you're safe and seated.

- **You're safe despite medical conditions.** If you're starting your exercises with pre-existing medical or physical conditions, you may be feeling hesitant to get into exercising. You may be unaware whether or not you have the strength to get through these exercises. Doing standing exercises may pose a threat, as you become dizzy or unbalanced, which causes a fall and painful injuries. By starting with seated exercises, you eliminate the threat of hurting yourself if you are facing physical and medical conditions that you're trying to overcome.

- **You don't strain your body.** Beside exercising with the reduced risk of falling, seated exercises are also valuable because they put less strain on your body. These exercises are quite simple and easy for your body, which means that you won't have to overly exert your body by doing exercises your muscles aren't prepared for. This will be a great way to introduce you to exercise because you will find it enjoyable instead of strenuous and overwhelming.
- **You can do a higher quantity of exercises.** Another benefit of doing seated exercises is being able to do a higher quantity of exercises. Because you're seated, you have more stamina to get through more exercises. These exercises are also less intense and strenuous, which means you can do a lot more of them without feeling fatigued.

We all have to start somewhere with our exercise journey. Seated exercises may seem too simple for you, but they're a great starting point for you to build onto. Once you practice these seated exercises consistently, you will see how it improves your overall fitness and health. Keep pushing yourself each day and soon, you will move on to other forms of exercises.

HOW TO DO EXERCISE IN A CHAIR

Before we go into the different beginner exercises you'll be practicing, let's discuss how you should go about exercising in a chair. You may be wondering to yourself how it's even possible to practice seated exercises in a chair. At this point of your exercising journey, your chair is going to be very beneficial. These are some practical tips that will ensure you have a successful and smooth workout with your chair of choice:

- **Wear the right clothing.** Earlier in the book it was suggested that you wear loose fitting clothing that doesn't restrict your movement, with that being said, you shouldn't wear clothing with fabric that is too loose to the point where it's a hazard. Hanging fabric can end up getting tangled in the chair which could provide a falling obstacle. So ensure that your clothing is more fitted, but not restrictive when you're doing seated exercises.
- **Use the right chair.** The chair that you use for your seated exercises is important, as it could make the difference between a safe workout and a risky one. You want to choose a stable chair that won't move as you work out, so avoid chairs with wheels or any infrastructure issues. For these exercises, it's more suitable to pick an armless chair, as the arms could be restrictive when you're trying to move around for each exercise.
- **Do not rush.** When you're practicing seated exercises, slow and steady will win the race. You may not enjoy

exercising, which causes you to rush through it. However, you will feel more benefits safely when you practice your exercises slowly. Move slowly with intention for each exercise so that you can experience the most from them. When you move slowly you will find that you reduce the risk of feeling dizzy or uncomfortable.

At the end of the day, practicing chair exercises is pretty safe and easy. Even if you do end up falling in your chair, which is very unlikely, you won't experience a serious injury. With this being said, you must still consider your safety. If you haven't exercised in a long time, your body will be a bit rusty, which means you can hurt yourself easily. If you feel anything hurting as you exercise, that's a sign that you must stop!

NECK AND HEAD MOBILITY EXERCISES

Now that you understand the basic rules and safety tips for seated exercises, we can dive into the physical activities you will be practicing. Although you are seated while doing these exercises, we want to work out every part of your body. Your balance and strength will be optimal when you exercise your whole body.

Let's start off by working out your neck and head area. Do you feel any tension in your neck and head as you sit? If you have a stiff neck that struggles to merely turn from side-to-side, these exercises will help. They will also help to relieve your headaches and back or shoulder pain you may be experiencing.

Exercise 1: Head Rolls

The first exercise you can do seated in your chair. This is a simple and effective exercise that will help to relieve tension from your neck. The head roll exercise is both a strength training exercise and a stretch, so it's perfect to start your workout with. These steps will help you to practice the head roll:

1. Look straight forward with your posture upright.
2. Move your chin toward your chest.
3. Tilt your head to your right gently.
4. Then roll your head to the back slowly.
5. Tilt your head to the left gently.
6. Return your chin to its position toward your chest.

You should repeat this motion five to ten times to get the true benefits from them. Be sure to roll your neck slowly, so you don't strain or hurt your neck muscles.

Exercise 2: Neck Releasing Pose

For this next neck exercise, you're going to practice a soothing yoga pose while seated. Seated yoga is a great way for you to stretch out and engage your muscles safely. You may find that your neck is so tense that it actually hurts when you roll it all the way around. If this is something uncomfortable for you, then you can opt to try this neck releasing activity instead.

For this activity, you are achieving the same purpose as the previous neck activity by stretching your neck to the side.

Doing this activity will release tension in your neck and shoulders. To practice this exercise, you must follow these steps:

1. Sit up in your chair and straighten your posture.
2. Ensure your feet are flat on the floor and stable.
3. Place your right hand on your right leg, while you reach your left arm over your head, placing it on the right side of your face.
4. Start to slowly push your right side of your face, then hold this position for 30 seconds.
5. Slowly lift your head back to your relaxed position and do the other side.
6. Place your left hand on your right leg, while you reach your right arm over your head, placing it on the left side of your face.
7. Slowly push your left side of your face, then hold this position for 30 seconds.
8. Slowly lift your head back to your relaxed position.

You can practice this exercise once on each side, as you're holding it for 30 seconds. This exercise will help to relieve the tension on the sides of your neck.

Exercise 3: Neck Stretch

This exercise is very similar to the previous two exercises. If you have practiced them, then you can sit this one out. However, if you haven't done the head roll exercise, you can go ahead and try this neck stretching exercise out instead! These are the following steps you can use to practice it successfully:

1. Get comfortable in your seat.
2. Put both hands on the back of your head and bring your elbows together.
3. With your hands you must push your head forward gently, until your chin touches your chest.
4. Hold this position for 30 seconds.

You can practice this exercise up to three times to experience the full stretch of your neck. Try to get your chin touching your chest, but if your neck is too stiff, you can get your neck as far down as it can go without any pain.

Exercise 4: Triceps Shoulder Stretch

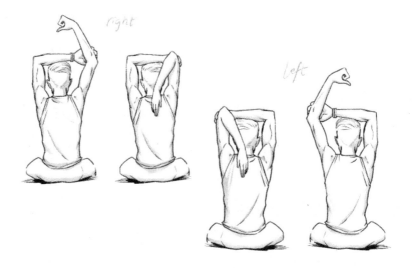

With this activity, you will be able to stretch your shoulders. There are various ways in which you can practice tricep shoulder stretches. For this exercise, we'll be exploring an over the shoulder tricep stretch. These steps will help you to practice this exercise:

1. Lengthen out your spine as you sit up straight.
2. Roll your shoulders backwards.

3. Reach your right arm up and then over your head until your hand is resting on the center of your back.

4. Use your left hand to gently push your arm further down, while it stays in the center.

5. You can hold it for thirty seconds and repeat this exercise for your left arm.

To receive the best results for this activity, you can practice it three to four times for each side. Ensure that you're gentle when you're pushing your arm down so that you don't strain any muscles.

Exercise 5: Shoulder Shrugs

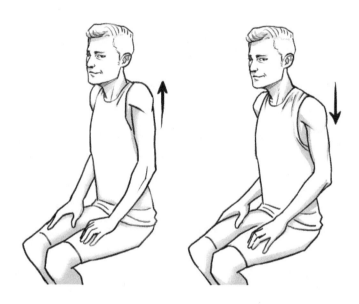

This next exercise is a movement that you're familiar with. When you don't know the answer to something, you may shrug your shoulders. This can actually be a form of exercise and stretching for your neck and shoulders. Although you may know how to shrug your shoulders, these are the steps to follow:

1. Sit up in your chair with your arms rested on your side.
2. Shrug your shoulders up to your ears, while leaning your shoulders backward.
3. Hold this position for 3 seconds.
4. Bring your shoulders forward and down, back to your resting position.

You can repeat this process ten times so that you can fully relax and stretch out your shoulder muscles. Don't forget to hold your shrugging position for each repetition.

BACK AND ARM STRENGTHENING EXERCISES

Next, we'll be looking into back and arm exercises that can help you to strengthen those important muscles. Unfortunately, as one gets older, they can lose a lot of their muscle mass. You may have had big muscles in your arms and backs when you were younger, but now it's like all that work you did back in the day has disappeared. Picking up heavy things may be challenging, or it may even end up hurting you. These exercises will help you to regain some muscles, as well as it will make using your arms and back less painful.

Exercise 6: Hand Stretches

If your bone density has been decreasing drastically, you may find yourself experiencing pain in your hands. Arthritis is a condition many seniors get when they struggle with their bone strength. If you experience pain and strain in your hands, this stretching exercise will help you drastically. Here are the steps to follow:

1. Start by putting your hands into a fist, and wrap your thumb around your knuckles.
2. Squeeze your fist gently and hold for 30 seconds.
3. You can then release and stretch your hand by spreading your fingers wide.
4. Repeat this four times for each hand.

Doing this activity will not only stretch your fingers out, but it will also make them stronger, as well as relieve any pain you may have.

Exercise 7: Grip Strengthener

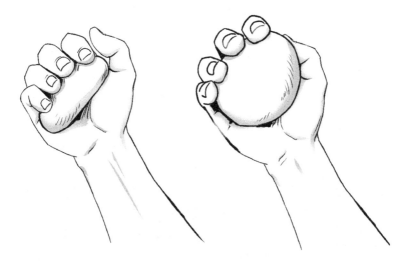

As your hands get more painful, you will find that they get weaker. You may have found that you drop objects a lot more easily because you don't have the grip strength you used to have. This exercise will help you to improve your grip strength, which will allow you to hold onto objects tightly. To improve your grips strength, practice the following steps:

1. Get a soft object like a stress ball.
2. Hold onto it as tight as you can for five seconds and then release.

3. You must repeat this fifteen times for each hand.
4. If it starts to feel easy to squeeze, then try squeeze harder and add more seconds as you hold.

After practicing this exercise frequently, you'll find it easier to hold and turn door knobs, carry heavier objects, and grip railings to prevent you from falling.

Exercise 8: Wrist Rotations

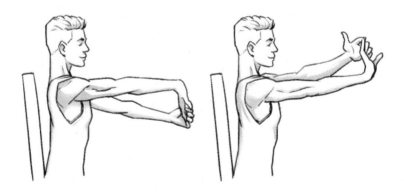

If you're struggling to move your wrist around normally because it's stiff and painful, practicing some wrist rotations may be just what you need to relieve this stiffness. These following steps will help you to successfully relax the tendons and ligaments in your wrist:

1. Stretch your right hand out in front of you, with your palm facing upward.
2. Point your fingers and palm downwards, until you feel a stretch.
3. Use your left hand to further pull down your hand and hold this position for five seconds.
4. You can then turn your arm around so that your palm is facing the ground.
5. Stretch your fingers upward toward the ceiling, until you feel a stretch in your hand and wrist.
6. You can use your left hand to further push your hand upwards and hold this position for five seconds.
7. Repeat this action three times and once you're done, relax your wrist and shake out your hand gently.
8. Repeat the above steps on your other hand three times as well.

After doing this, your wrist will feel a lot less tense and stiff, which will help you to perform other exercises.

Exercise 9: Desk Press

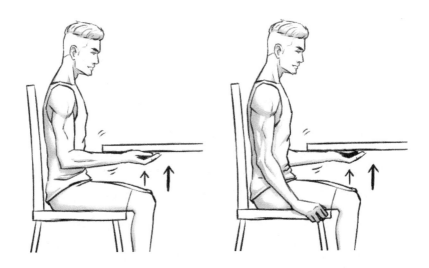

If you're unable to perform everyday tasks because you have a stiffness in your wrists that holds you back. This exercise will help to stretch both your wrist and your forearm. You can follow these steps:

1. As you're seated, use a desk or table for this activity.
2. Sit close to the table, so you can place one hand under it.
3. Ensure your palm is facing upwards as you make contact with the bottom of the table.
4. Press upwards into the desk (you should be feeling the pressure in your wrist and forearm).
5. Hold this position for up to ten seconds.

6. Then repeat this exercise with your other arm under the table.

This exercise is great for strengthening muscles between your elbows and wrists.

Exercise 10: Windshield Wiper Wrist Movement

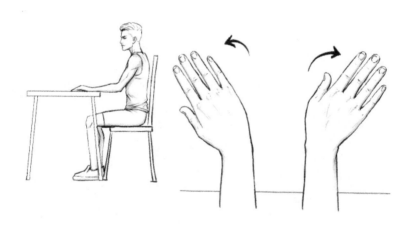

Be seated at a desk or table for this activity. You will be stretching your wrist through the following steps:

1. Place your hand facing palm down on the table in front of you.
2. Start by pointing your hand to the right without moving your wrist or arm, and hold for three seconds.

3. Then point your hand to the left without moving your wrist, and hold for three seconds.

4. Repeat this three times for each hand.

This will help relieve tension or pain you may have been experiencing in your wrists by stretching them out.

Exercise 11: Torso and Shoulder Release

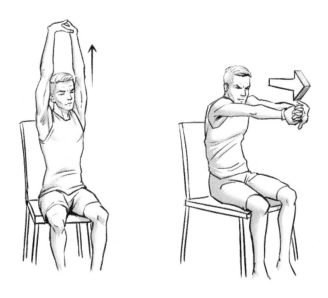

For this exercise, we're going to target your shoulders and torso. There are many ways for you to release the tension in your shoulders and torso. Firstly, in this exercise you will focus on releasing your torso and shoulders, by following these steps:

1. Lift your arms above your head and interlock your fingers with your palm facing upwards.

2. Push your palms upwards in five small pulses.
3. You can then bring your arms down.
4. Repeat this five times.

Now you can move on to the second part of this exercise where you focus on an upper back opener. Continue to follow these steps:

1. Reach your arms out in front of you with your fingers interlocked and your palm facing outwards.
2. Push your palms out in the form of five short pulses.
3. Round your back as you do this, with your chin tucked in.
4. You can move your hands side to side while you're in this position to open up your back as much as possible.
5. After ten seconds of this, lower your hands and return to your relaxed seated position.

As with the first part of this exercise, you can practice this five times to feel the stretch in your upper back.

Exercise 12: Torso Twist

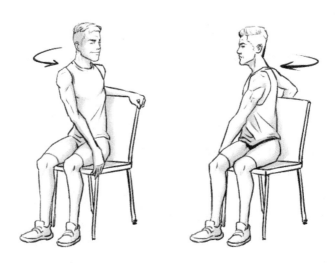

While seated, it can be challenging to target your torso, but this exercise will do the trick. If you find yourself slouching badly, having spinal issues, back pain, and a stiff upper body, this torso twist exercise will help you. Follow these steps to practice it:

1. Sit up straight with your spine straightened up as much as possible.
2. Your feet must be placed flat and firmly on the ground.
3. Turn your torso to the right as though you're trying to turn around and look at something.
4. Place both of your hands at the right hand side of the back of your chair to get a full stretch.

5. Hold this position for five seconds and then turn back to your relaxed pose slowly.
6. You can then repeat on your left side and hold for five seconds.
7. Repeat this exercise three times for each side.

When you're practicing this activity, please be sure to do it slowly and gently. You don't want to end up getting hurt.

Exercise 13: Spinal Stretch

For this exercise, you will be able to successfully stretch out your whole spine, which can be extremely relieving if you have bad posture and back pain. Here's how you can do it:

1. As you inhale deeply, lift your arms up above your head.

2. When you exhale round your torso forward,

3. Lean forward as if you were picking something up on the floor in front of you. This will let your spine round out.

4. Ensure that your neck is relaxed as you hold this position for five seconds.

5. After holding it, inhale deeply so you can roll up slowly and lift your arms to repeat this same motion.

6. You can do this five times.

Exercise 14: Backbend and Chest Opener

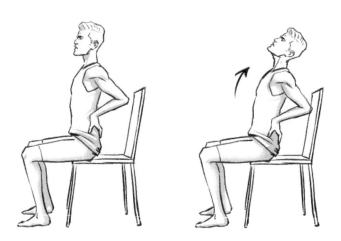

This exercise will help you to open up your chest and relieve tension in your upper and lower back. Before starting, be sure you relax your entire body, as it may require you to be more

flexible than you're used to. Follow these instructions to practice this exercise successfully:

1. Sit a bit forward on your chair so that there's some
   room behind you.
2. Place your hands on your lower back or on your hips,
   whichever is more comfortable for you.
3. As you inhale deeply, you must lift your chest and lift
   your chin up.
4. While doing this your shoulders must open up,
   allowing your chest to expand.
5. Hold this position for ten seconds and as you exhale,
   slowly move back into your relaxed seated position.
6. Repeat this activity three times.

After all of these exercises, your torso and entire upper body
should be feeling a lot less tense. Your muscles feel more
engaged, as you've stretched most of them out. The more you
practice them, the easier they will feel for you.

LEGS, HAMSTRINGS, HIP, AND FEET EXERCISES

The legs, hamstrings and hips are the base of your balance and
mobility. To get and keep this part of your body strong and
limber, it is crucial to the wellbeing of your quality of life to
include exercises that accomplish this.

For the lower half of your body, we are targeting many
different muscles and ligaments. Some people in their later
years may have a hard time walking around, getting upstairs,

standing up and sitting down, or moving with ease, these exercises are targeted to those activities.

When your mobility worsens, it's often due to your hips, legs, and feet that have not been properly stretch and the strengthened. When you target these aspects of your body with exercise, you will see a dramatic improvement in your mobility. Having strong legs will prevent you from falling, and if you do fall, you're less likely to have a severe injury.

Exercise 15: Single Leg Bend Forward

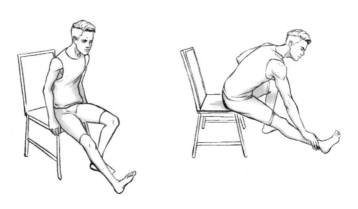

You want to be able to target your legs and all of the muscles in them like your hamstrings, glutes, and your calves without having to stand up and putting too much pressure and weight on your legs. This exercise will stretch your hamstrings and it helps to improve your balance. This is how you do it:

1. Sit on the edge of your seat, ensure that you have enough balance and stability, so you don't fall off of your chair.
2. Stretch your right leg out in front of you.
3. Inhale and straighten out your back so that you're sitting tall.
4. As you exhale, roll your torso forward and reach your arms out, holding onto the leg that is extended.
5. Move your arms as far down as you can and hold it there for a few breaths.
6. As you exhale, move back up, and then repeat this exercise three more times.
7. Now do the above steps for your left leg.

You know you're doing this exercise successfully when you're able to feel the stretch in your hamstrings. Don't push yourself if it's too painful, but a little bit of pain means you are stretching your muscles.

Exercise 16: Hamstring Stretch

For this exercise you may need to get a belt or a strong scarf. This is a seated yoga position that will also strengthen your calves and abdominal muscles, which will ultimately improve your balance:

1. Make a loop in your belt or scarf, hold onto both ends of it in your right hand, as you put your right foot into the loop.
2. Push your right leg as far out as you can, while your foot pulls the strap you're holding onto tightly.
3. Keep your back straight as you straighten your right leg.
4. As you're in this position, point your toes to flex your leg muscles.

5. Do this five times and then hold your position for five seconds.

6. After this, slowly lower your belt or strap and then lower your right leg.

7. Now repeat this exercise on your left leg.

When you do this exercise, keep your leg straight, but if you have to bend your knee to feel more comfortable, that's okay. You can repeat this exercise two to three times for each leg.

Exercise 17: Glute Stretch - Chair Pigeon Pose

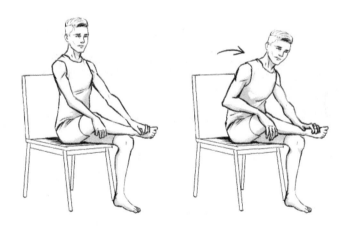

Now, let's move onto exercising your glutes. You may be wondering how it's possible for you to work out your glutes when you're sitting on them, but this is the perfect exercise that will stretch these muscles. It's a yoga pose that can be practiced seated through the following steps:

1. Sit a bit forward on your chair, so half of the chair is open behind you.
2. Lift your right leg and cross your right ankle over your left knee.
3. In this position, you can gently move your knee up and down. Do this five times.
4. Stay in this position as you inhale and fold your spine forward, holding this position for a few seconds.
5. Then exhale, straightening your back and placing your right foot back on the floor.
6. Repeat this two times for each leg.

This exercise is not only valuable to help you stretch these muscles, but it also allows you to open up your hips.

Exercise 18: Seated Hero's Pose

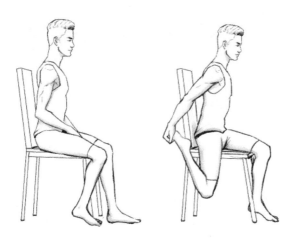

For this exercise, you will be targeting the large quadriceps in your front thighs and your hips. It's a great exercise to work your muscles that are tight from sitting for extended periods of time. Although you're doing seated exercises, you want to be able to stretch out your body as you sit down. Follow these steps to practice it:

1. Scoot over to the slide of the chair, until your right leg is off the chair.
2. Hold the other edge of your chair with your left hand so that you're able to balance.
3. Once you're holding on and you feel stable in your chair, start to lean your right foot backwards.

4. Bring the heel of your right foot as close to your buttock as possible and then hold onto your foot with your right hand.
5. Hold this position for 15 seconds as you feel the stretch in your muscles in front of your thigh.
6. Let go slowly and then shift over to the other side of the chair to practice the same exercise with your left leg.

You will bend your legs backwards as far as they let you, and don't push your leg if you feel any pain in your leg muscles.

Exercise 19: Leg Circles

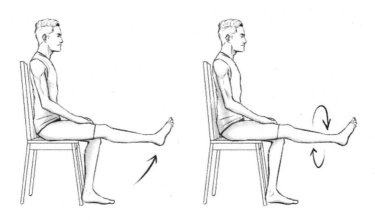

This exercise is a great way for you to stretch your muscles, while strengthening them at the same time. Here's how to perform it:

1. Sit comfortably in your chair.
2. Lift your right leg up until it's in line with your hip.
3. Without moving your hip, start doing clockwise circles with your right leg.
4. Do this for 20 seconds, or as long as you can working your way up to 20 seconds, and then put your foot down.
5. Repeat this movement with your left leg.
6. Do this three times for each leg.

You can make your circles as small or wide as you'd like. The wider you make the circle, the more uncomfortable and straining it may feel.

Exercise 20: Glute Squeeze

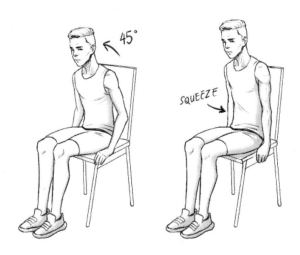

To give your glute muscles some extra attention, do this squeezing activity. This will help you to focus on your glutes, as you fully engage these muscles. This is how to practice this simple yet effective exercise:

1. While in your chair, lean forward at a 45-degree angle.
2. Place your hands on your lap.
3. Engage your glutes by squeezing them in as you count to three and then release.
4. Do this 15 to 20 times to really feel your muscle engagement.

You may feel the tension in your glutes disappear after practicing this exercise a couple times. You may struggle to squeeze them fully at first, but with practice it will be more effective.

Exercise 21: Seated March

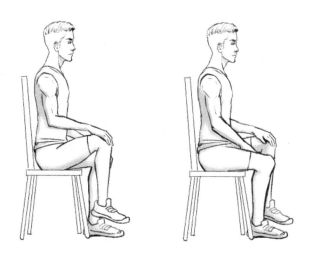

For this seated exercise, we will practice an exercise that will get your blood flowing. It can be challenging to get your blood circulating and your heart pumping when you're seated, but this exercise will help you to accomplish this when you follow these steps:

1. Sit up straight in your chair with your feet flat on the floor.
2. Lift up one knee at a time as though you are marching in one place.

3. Do this march for about a minute.
4. As you do it, keep your core engaged.
5. You can start lifting your knees higher and practicing this exercise faster the more skilled you become.

Do this exercise for as long and as fast as you would like to. Try to push yourself until you feel like you're breaking a sweat.

HOW OFTEN YOU SHOULD BE PRACTICING THESE EXERCISES

These are all the seated exercises that are suggested for you to practice. If you are wondering how frequent you should practice these activities for them to be effective and helpful, keep in mind that when you're exercising, it's crucial for you to have rest days that help you replenish your strength and energy and let your muscles grow.

However, these seated exercises are a lot less intense than normal exercises. These are less intense, and they act as stretches and muscle wakeners. You're simply activating and engaging muscles.

It's best to practice these five to six days in a week. You need to choose one or two rest days that can help your muscles to recover and strengthen. Although you must make time for rest days, you must keep your exercise consistent. The more you practice them, the more you prepare your body to move on to more challenging and intensive exercises!

On the days that you are not doing exercise it is good to do stretches on those days. Use the same time of day you do exercises to do stretches. This will also help keep your routine and exercise habit in place. Every day you will be making progress.

6

STANDING EXERCISES

"If you don't make time for exercise, you'll probably have to make time for illness."

— ROBIN SHARMA

Once you've conquered the sitting down exercises and you feel more comfortable and mobile, you can pursue some standing exercises. These will use more force and help you to develop some physical resilience. We will cover various exercises that will help different muscle groups and improve your strength and balance.

LEVELING UP THE INTENSITY

Once you see and feel the progress in your fitness from the seated exercises and they become comfortable to do, it's time for you to pursue standing ones. Seating exercises are a valuable starting point, but you won't see as much growth and improvement in your mobility if you don't move onto standing exercises. So good job on accomplishing what you have accomplished so far. It's time to level up!

Benefits of Standing Exercises

Once you start standing exercises, you may find it challenging, but you'll experience far more benefits than you will with seated exercises. You will experience the most progress and benefits when you practice standing exercises consistently. These are some of the benefits you will experience form standing exercises:

- **Challenges your muscles.** Standing exercises can be very challenging for your muscles. This challenge will promote healthy growth and strength within your body. You use more effort to do standing exercises. You will find after your standing exercise you feel stronger because your muscles have been challenged.
- **Your balance improves.** One of the main reasons why standing exercises are so valuable is because they give you the opportunity to practice balancing and the muscles you use to balance. As you stand and practice exercises, it forces your body to focus on balancing. You

need to be able to use your whole body to keep you grounded and stable as you practice each activity.

- **Experiencing massive progress.** Of course, the main reason why you're participating in these exercises is for you to see progress in your health and fitness. As you progress you will see the difference in your mobility, strength, and balance as all three of these will grow together and improve your quality of life.

The more you practice standing exercises, the better you're going to feel. You will experience all the health benefits of exercise when you practice standing up. Don't be afraid to push yourself out of your comfort zone. You may not be used to these types of exercises, but with time you will get the hang of them. And it's worth it. Keep in mind why you decided to get fit in the first place.

Take it on a gradient

Now that you're leveling up to standing exercises, you need to be more precautious. Be in control of your actions and movements. If you haven't done any standing up exercise in a long while, you need to pace yourself. If you push yourself too hard and get hurt, you'll possibly end up deterring yourself from exercising again. These are some tips that will help you to be easy on yourself so that you don't overwork your mind and body:

- **Have rest days.** Although it's crucial for you to be consistent when you're exercising, you also want to maintain a healthy level of exercise and rest. Our bodies will always need rest, which means that it's valuable for you to take time off to relax and rest your body every now and then. When you exercise hard every single day without taking breaks, not only will you burn out, but you also increase your risk of injury.

- **Stop when you feel pain or discomfort.** When you start practicing standing exercises, you need to understand your body better. This means that you need to be aware of your body's limits so that you don't end up hurting yourself or experiencing extreme fatigue. Knowing your body will help you to stop when you're feeling unexplainable pain or discomfort.

- **Don't get disheartened.** You're starting off with standing. Unfortunately, you're most likely not going to be as fit as you may want to be. You may have to sit down between exercises, or you have to shorten the amount of exercises you can do. Don't be hard on yourself when you don't exercise how you may have wanted to. The best solution to avoid this from happening is by starting with exercises within your capabilities and building onto them gradually!

- **Don't rush.** You may be feeling excited and motivated to workout at a fast pace. Although it's great to have this burst of energy, you need to be able to exercise at a steady pace. It may feel natural for you to rush through each exercise, but doing this can actually put you in danger. You need to practice each exercise thoughtfully and steadily. This will not only keep you safe as you exercise, but it will also help you to engage your muscles with more intent.

Ultimately, this exercising journey should be enjoyable and life changing for you. In order for you to have a positive experience, you need to both push yourself and be easy on yourself. This may sound contradictory and impossible, but it's possible if you work hard gradually and slowly to reach your fitness goals. You start off with less intense exercises, and build onto them as you get stronger and fitter!

CHAIR LEANING ACTIVITIES

Once you've successfully nailed all of the seated exercises and you may feel like challenging yourself a little, you can start practicing exercises where you use your chair for other purposes. Getting off the chair to practice some exercises will increase the intensity of your workout, while still remaining safe as you use the chair as a prop to lean on. These are some chair leaning exercises you can try out if you're feeling more confident in your body.

Exercise 22: Chair Yoga Lunge Pose

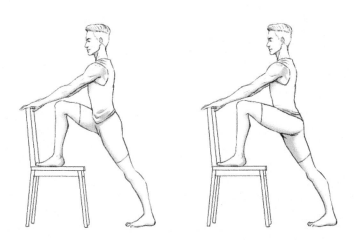

The lunge pose is a very effective yoga position that will help you to stretch out your leg muscles. Doing it as a chair pose is valuable for you if you experience knee discomfort, as it allows you to perform the same exercise without overexerting yourself. Here's how you practice the chair yoga lunge:

1. Get up from the chair and stand an arm's length away from the front of it.
2. Step your left foot onto the chair and put all of your weight into this leg.
3. Lean forward and you should feel a stretch in your calves.
4. Your left knee should be above your foot, not in front of it.

5. Hold this position for fifteen seconds and then you can let go.
6. Now return to your starting position and repeat this activity with your right leg.

Do this for however long you feel comfortable with. If you find that your balance is an issue, you can turn your chair to the side so that you hold onto the back of the chair as you practice the lunge.

Exercise 23: Half-Splits Pose

For this exercise, you may have to practice some flexibility. Before you get scared of the title of this exercise, don't worry because you're not doing the splits. To do this exercise you can follow through directly after you do the previous exercise with your right foot up on the chair in the lunge position. From this position, you will perform the half-splits pose with a chair using the following steps:

1. From the lunge position, you must straighten the leg out that is on the chair.
2. Rest your heel on the chair.
3. Walk your hands down this leg that is on the chair.
4. Your hips should open up and bend forward as you do this.
5. Hold this position for fifteen seconds.
6. Return your leg to a standing position and then switch legs and do the same thing for fifteen seconds.

Doing this exercise will stretch out your legs safely, as you're able to maintain your balance.

Exercise 24: Single Limb Stance

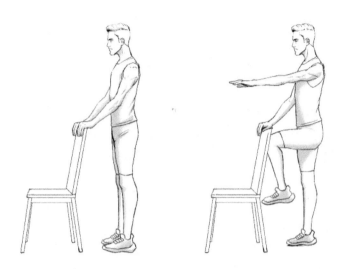

If you find yourself struggling to balance while doing these standing exercises with a chair, it's valuable to use this exercise to practice your balancing skills. Following these steps will help you to exercise your legs and your balancing abilities:

1. Stand behind your chair.
2. Hold your right arm on the back of the chair and ensure that your right foot is stood firmly and flat on the ground.
3. Lift your left leg up, while lifting up your left arm to stabilize yourself.
4. Stay balanced as you bring your right foot down and then switch off to your other leg. Now holding the back of the chair with your left had as you rase your left leg.

Your goal should be to stay in this position for approximately one minute, but you can do it for as long as it's comfortable for you. You may need to start off with less time holding up your leg, so, take it on a gradient.

WALL EXERCISES

Wall exercises are when you practice standard exercises, but instead of doing them standing up on your own, you lean on the wall for support. For these exercises, your back will be leaning on the wall as you do standing exercises. This is a great way for you to engage your muscles, while avoiding putting too much strain on them.

It's also valuable because it prevents an element of fear that may be worrying you. When you lean on the wall while exercising, you are less likely to fall and get hurt. If you feel yourself starting to lose balance and fall, then you put more pressure on the wall so that you don't topple over. You can do many exercises using the wall that makes you more comfortable. Here are a few specific wall exercises to do.

Exercise 25: Wall Pushups

We all know that push-ups are a great way for you to strengthen your upper body, but just like anything else, your muscles need to be developed to the strength to do them. This is why it's valuable for you to let gravity help you by practicing wall push-ups. This is how you successfully practice pushups by using a wall:

1. Stand with your feet at hip-width apart, while you're three feet away from the wall.
2. Lean forward until your hands lie flat on the wall in front of you and ensure that your arms are aligned with your shoulders.
3. Move your body toward the wall and then use your arms to push yourself back to your original position.

4. Repeat this motion 10 times.

This exercise will help you to feel the burn in your arm muscles, as you push your body weight against the wall.

Exercise 26: Wall Squats

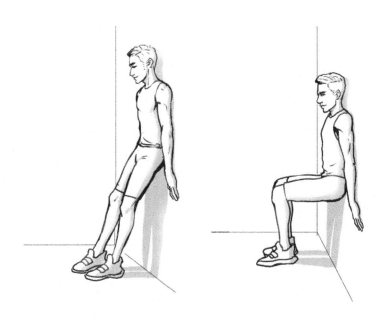

If you'd like to strengthen your lower body, then squats are a great way for you to accomplish this. This wall squat is also known as a wall sit. If bending your knees is painful for you and causes you to lose your balance, then practicing wall squats will help you to bend with more ease. Here is how you perform this exercise:

1. Lean your back against the wall with your feet two feet away from the wall.

2. Slowly slide your back down the wall, as far down as you can go.

3. Stop sliding down when your thighs are parallel to the ground.

4. Ensure that your knees align with your ankles.

5. Hold this position for 20 seconds and then slide back up.

6. Rest for 30 seconds and then repeat this exercise three times.

If this exercise is a bit challenging for you, start off holding the squat position (in step 5 above) for 5 or 10 seconds at a time and work your way up to 20 seconds. Take it easy and work your way up gradually.

Exercise 27: Wall Planks

A great way for you to simply strengthen your core is by practicing some wall planks. These are similar to wall pushups but instead of pushing yourself up, you will hold yourself at an angle by tightening your core. Follow these steps to practice the wall planks:

1. Stand three feet from the wall.
2. Reach your arms out so that your palms touch the wall.
3. Lower your body toward the wall until both forearms are on the wall.
4. Ensure that your arm muscles are engaged.
5. Keep your core muscles engaged in this position and hold for fifteen seconds.

6. You can then push yourself up, take a 30 second rest, and then repeat two more times.

OTHER STANDING EXERCISES

Now that your body is feeling stronger and more prepared to practice standing exercises, we're going to level up the intensity. These standing exercises will target all of the muscles in your body, without balancing on a wall or chair. As it strengthens you physically, it will also improve your balancing skills.

Exercise 28: Heel Lifts

When doing standing exercises, it's easier for you to target your legs. For this exercise, you'll be working out your calves. This exercise will also help you to strengthen your balance, as you aren't using a chair or wall to support your body weight. Here is how you practice this exercise:

1. Stand up straight with your arms lifted to the side.
2. Raise yourself on your toes as high as you can go and then relax your legs and lower yourself.
3. Repeat this motion 10-15 times, take a small break and then continue to do another 10-15 reps.

If you feel as though this exercise is too difficult to do without something to lean on, you can use the back of the chair by holding onto it as you do your toe lifts.

Exercise 29: Sit to Stand

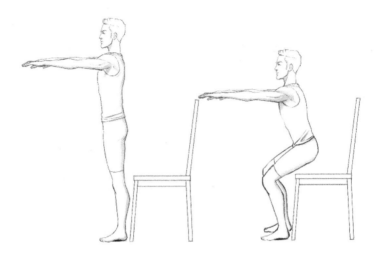

The number of different muscles you use to stand up and sit down would amaze you. The average person will use around 300 different muscles just to stand. Standing up can be a challenging task, and this is what makes the Sit to Stand exercise so valuable. Here are the steps to perform this exercise.

1. Stand up in front of your chair with your legs slightly apart.
2. Hold your arms out in front of you for balance.
3. Bend your knees as you lower your body toward the seat.
4. Pause for a beat and then engage your leg and core muscles as you return to your standing position.

This type of exercise will work out your legs as you are essentially doing a type of squatting motion. Start of doing the Sit to Stand exercise 5 times. As you progress work your way up to doing 20 at a time.

Exercise 30: Clock Reach

For this exercise, you must pretend like your body is a clock. You're going to need to maintain a certain level of balance, as this is an exercise you do on one leg. Here's how you do this exercise:

1. Stand with your feet firmly on the ground.
2. Lift your right foot, so you're balancing on your left leg.
3. With your right arm do circles motions as if it was a clock arm.

4. Start with your arm at 12 o'clock which is above your head.

5. Then slowly swing your arm toward 6 o'clock behind you.

If you find that you struggle to balance throughout this activity, you can choose to use a chair to lean on as you practice it. You could also do the same actions with both feet on the ground and then work toward doing it on one leg.

Exercise 31: Tree Pose

This is a yoga pose you can practice that will strengthen your thighs and your calves. The aim of this exercise is for you to feel rooted and stable. It can help with your posture, as well as it relieves pains in your joints, specifically in your ankles. This is how you go about practicing this pose:

1. Stand with your feet close together.
2. Engage your leg muscles as you press your feet into the ground.
3. Inhale and lift your chest while bringing your hands on your hips.
4. Once you feel balanced, you can lift your left leg and place your foot as high up on your right inner thigh as possible.
5. Hold this position for a few seconds.
6. If you're feeling steady, lift your arms straight up over your head as you inhale deeply.
7. Hold this position for another few seconds.
8. You can then return to your relaxed position and then repeat this movement with your right leg.

To ensure that you don't fall in this position, you must ensure that your hips are open. Your knees should only be slightly facing outward.

HOW OFTEN SHOULD YOU DO STANDING EXERCISES

Once you're doing more intensive, standing exercises, you need to create a proper schedule for yourself. This form of exercise can be a bit more strenuous, which can make it easier for you to give up and take lots of days off. If you want to see real results in your health and fitness, you need to be able to practice consistency. If you're struggling to figure out how frequently you should exercise and how to motivate yourself to do so, you should consider the following:

- **Stick to schedules.** When you get started with this journey, you will find different exercises that you enjoy. Once you know what works for you and your body, it's so important for you to create a schedule for you to stick to. Creating a daily exercise plan will help you to stay accountable, which motivates consistency and drive. It's all about creating that healthy habit to improve your quality of life.
- **Allocating different muscle movements for different days.** You want to avoid exercising the same parts of your body every day. This can be very tedious and tiresome for your muscles. This makes it valuable to schedule different exercises for each day of the week. Like upper body one day and legs and hips the next.
- **Have rest days.** Because standing exercises are more intensive than the previous seated exercises, you must have rest days. If you don't rest your body at least once a week, it could cause you to burnout or injure yourself. You need to give yourself the necessary rest to let your muscles grow and rebuild. On the days you rest it is a good idea to do stretches on those days. Stretching will help keep your body limber and not as stiff from the previous day's work out.

To be successful with these exercises, you need to be consistent while still listening to your body. You will see the results when you exercise frequently during the week. You also need to relax your muscles so that they can grow and strengthen.

7

WALKING FOR HEALTH

"No matter how slow you go you're still lapping everyone on the couch."

— SUSIE MILLER

One of the easiest and best ways for you to work on your physical health and mobility is by walking every day. By integrating walking into your life on a regular basis, you can drastically improve your physical health and mobility. Here are some walking exercises that you can at home.

BENEFITS OF WALKING

We can often forget how truly valuable walking is for our health. It's something we do everyday without even thinking about it in depth. The more you walk each day, the healthier you will be. You can prevent yourself from aging rapidly by taking sufficient steps on a daily basis. Here are some of the benefits you get from walking:

- **Improves heart health.** One of the major benefits of walking that you should consider is its benefit on your heart health. As you get older, your cardiac health drastically decreases. Your risk of a heart attack or stroke increases the older you get, and it's a common cause of death. When you do cardio, walking, running, or cycling, it works out your heart as well, which makes it fitter and healthier.
- **Improves your balance.** If you find yourself dizzy, light-headed, and unbalanced when you stand up and walk, walking more as a form of exercise will eliminate this issue. You also become stronger, as your muscles strengthen throughout your body, which ultimately helps you to balance better. The more you walk, the less

trouble you will have balancing in your everyday life. Being able to balance with ease will reduce your risk of falling and getting hurt.

- **Improves bone density.** As we've established earlier, when your body gets older the bone density decreases, making your body more fragile. Walking makes your bones stronger, as well as it improves the strength of your ligaments and muscles. Consistently walking will reduce your chances of getting osteoporosis or arthritis.
- **Boosts energy and stamina.** Some people may be struggling to get into exercising because their energy levels are always low. They can feel unmotivated to do exercises on a daily basis because they are too tired to get started. You will find a major boost in your energy when you walk more, which will improve your quality of life. Practicing the activities that make you happy is a lot easier when you don't get as fatigued.
- **Weight loss.** Another benefit of walking is weight loss. Walking for 30 minutes a day is great. But every minute you walk past that 30 minutes you start to burn stored fat.
- **Helps your mental health.** One of the biggest reasons why walking is so beneficial for you is that it improves your mental health. If you're struggling with depression or anxiety, getting your blood flowing through your body by walking will help you greatly. Getting out in nature and walking can clear your mind, helping you to manage your anxiety and depression by releasing your attention outward. It also helps you mentally as it provides you with the opportunity to socialize with

new people. Meeting people can help you to combat your feelings of loneliness and isolation.

Walking is a really great way for you to exercise and improve your fitness. When you add walking to your schedule, you will find that it helps you to accomplish the other exercises in this book.

HOW TO MOTIVATE YOURSELF TO WALK

You may enjoy walking every now and then, but you may struggle to get yourself to walk on a daily basis. You can begin to feel lazy and not want to get yourself out of your comfortable bed or chair to walk outdoors. To experience the benefits of walking, you need to be able to push yourself so you can walk consistently. These following tips will keep you motivated to work on a daily basis:

- **Embrace nature.** One of the best ways to motivate yourself to keep on walking is by finding an enjoyable route that you want to walk daily. Embrace nature by going for walks in the park, by a lake, or the beach if you live close to one. Being in a natural and vibrant setting can make your walking feel like it's not even exercise. This will encourage you to feel excited to walk every day.
- **Get a walking partner.** It can be challenging to feel motivated and push yourself every day, that's what makes it valuable for you to get a walking partner. You may allow yourself to slack off, but having a walking

partner that holds you accountable will push you to walk daily. It's good to have a set time you meet up every day at a certain time for your daily walk. Having a walking partner will also make you more excited to workout every day.

- **Keep a comfortable pace.** When we say you should walk for exercise, this doesn't mean you must be an intense speed walker. Yes, in order to make it an exercise you must speed up your pace so that it's not a Sunday stroll. However, you can keep any type of pace that feels comfortable for you. When you walk at a comfortable pace that's fast enough to break a little sweat, but not too fast that it makes you too sore to get out of bed the next day.

- **Set goals.** Another way for you to stay motivated is by setting practical walking goals for yourself. You can set goals by having a specific amount of steps you want to accomplish in a day, the specific landmark you want to reach, or how long you want to walk for. Having these set goals that you strive to achieve everyday will push you to walk on a daily basis. You will impress yourself by continuously accomplishing your walking goals.

Once you find what drives your passion to walk, you will find yourself being more consistent than ever. Having something positive that drives you will ultimately get you the benefits you desire.

WALKING EXERCISES

When you think of walking, you may envision yourself going for a stroll in a park, but walking can be explored in an alternative way. If you don't feel prepared or ready to go walking outside because you're concerned about how much you can handle and whether it's safe for you to be moving around by yourself, you can look into practicing walking exercises. These types of exercises allow you to receive the benefits of walking, without risking your fall safety. Also there will be the occasional rainy days, so keeping in a walking schedule at home will keep you fit and progressing towards your health goals.

Although it's valuable to get started with walking exercises, the main goal is walking outdoors. here are some walking exercises that can inspire you to walk more.

Exercise 32: Marching on The Spot

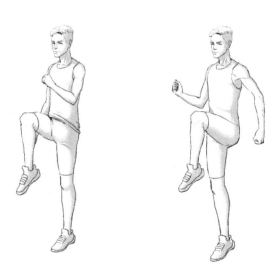

For this exercise, you will do something similar to the seated exercise. Instead of just marching your legs as you sit down, you will now march with your whole body on the spot. This exercise is great for you if you want to walk but you're not ready to walk in external environments yet. You're able to get the benefits of marching in the comfort of your own home. This is how you can practice marching on the spot successfully:

1. Stand comfortably with your two feet flat, hip-width apart.
2. Lift your right leg up, until your knee is at hip level.
3. Put your right leg down and then lift your left leg up.
4. Keep alternating your legs and as you do this move your arms along with your legs.

5. Do this marching motion for ten to fifteen minutes.

At first, you may struggle to lift your leg to hip level while maintaining your balance, so try to lift your legs as high up as possible. You can practice this near a wall or chair to prevent yourself from falling if you lose balance. Also, take it on a gradient. If you need to start off doing only a few minutes at a time, that's okay. Just keep working on it and your stamina will improve and you'll be able to increase the amount of time you can perform this exercise.

Exercise 33: Weighted Walking

Once you've tackled marching on the spot, you can continue to do some walking on the spot but intensify it by adding some weights. For this exercise you can get some weights that you can carry easily, or you could use ankle weights that are made for walking. Here's how you do the weighted walking exercise:

1. Find a safe spot in your home to walk in.
2. Start walking on the spot and get to a comfortable pace.
3. You can then pick up your weights or attach ankle weights to your ankles.
4. Keep the weights in your hands (or strapped to your ankles) and move your arms naturally up and down as you walk.
5. Try this weighted walking for five to ten minutes.

As you get more comfortable with this exercise, you can add more weight to your walk. You could also walk longer or walk on the spot on an incline to really challenge yourself.

Exercise 34: Walking Heel to Toe

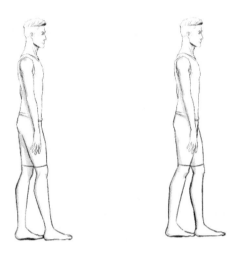

If your balance is something you're struggling with when you're walking, then this is an exercise you should do. This helps you to walk in a line, which strengthens your legs and cores. Practicing this exercise will prevent you from falling when you walk. This is how you can practice heel to toe walking:

1. Stand on even ground with lots of space in front of you.
2. Place your left foot in front of your right foot.
3. Ensure that the toes of your left foot are touching the heel of your right foot.
4. Then, lift your right foot and put your heel in front of your left foot's toes.
5. Keep on putting one foot in front of the other in this manner as you move forward.

6. Walk like this for 15-20 steps.

When you're doing this exercise, it can be easy for you to put all your focus on your feet. This may distract you from your surroundings, which can cause you to fall or lose balance. You need to make sure that you are aware of your surroundings as you practice this exercise.

TIPS FOR WALKING

After you've gathered your strength and confidence in your ability to walk in an external environment, you can now work toward walking on a daily basis to get your steps in. Getting out and walking will be extremely beneficial for your health, which will help you reduce your fall risk drastically. But, before you get out of the house and walk, you must take some tips into consideration:

- **Pick up the pace.** When you start walking, you may find that you get into the habit of going at a snail's pace. You walk around how you're used to, which doesn't really help you to break a sweat. You need to be able to pick up the pace because this is an exercise, not a Sunday stroll. This doesn't mean you must start speed walking straight away; it just means you should walk with a purpose.
- **Stretching before and after.** Before starting on your daily walk, it is important to do same basic stretches to limber up your joints, ligaments, and muscles. This will also help wake up the body and prevent any injuries

from pulling a tight muscle. Then again, do stretches at the end of your walk. This will also help to keep your joints, ligaments and muscles limber as you cool down from your walk.

- **Walk in the right conditions.** As a senior, you need to be cautious when you go for a walk. You can't just walk in any type of weather condition because this could become a hazardous safety issue for you. Only walk during the day and avoid walking at night by all means because you won't be able to see properly. You must also avoid walking during the rain or bad weather conditions, as you may slip and fall, ending up getting hurt.

You want to ensure walking is a comfortable experience for you so that you don't end up injuring yourself. This is why it's valuable to follow these tips, as well as some others such as carrying water with you, letting family and friends know when you're walking and where. Also walking a route that you know is also a good idea.

CREATE YOUR OWN WALKING PROGRAM

If you practice some of the previous walking exercises and they feel like the perfect fit for you, you should create a walking program for yourself. You may find that walking makes you happier and provides you with great benefits. By creating a walking program for yourself, you're able to explore a consistent fitness journey.

A walking plan is a week-by-week schedule that you create for yourself. Having a plan will help you to stay consistent, as it motivates you to stay on the right track. This is just an example of a walking program that you could use for your fitness journey or for inspiration to create your own schedule.

Week 1

For week one, you can start with some less intense exercises, to slowly introduce yourself to walking. This is important as you want to progress on a gradient and build up your strength, balance, and endurance. This is what your first week may look like.

Monday

- Stretch for two minutes.
- Low intense walk for five to ten minutes.
- Stretch for one minute.
- Low intense walk for five to ten minutes.

Tuesday

- Stretch for two minutes.
- Low intense stroll for ten to fifteen minutes.
- Stretch for two minutes.

Wednesday

- Stretch for two minutes.
- Low intense walk for five to ten minutes.
- Stretch for one minute.
- Low intense walk for five to ten minutes.

Thursday

- Stretch for two minutes.
- Low intense stroll for ten to fifteen minutes.
- Stretch for two minutes.

Friday

- Rest day! It is good to do stretches on your rest day.

Weekend

- Walking on the weekend is optional.
- Low intense stroll for 15-20 minutes.
- Window shop!

Week 2

Week two will be very similar to week one, as you need to ease yourself into this journey. However, there should be some gradual leveling up in the intensity so that you can increase your fitness overtime. This is how you could structure your second week of walking for exercise.

Monday

- Stretch for two minutes.
- Low intense walk for five to ten minutes.
- Stretch for two minutes.
- Brisk walk for five to ten minutes.

Tuesday

- Stretch for two minutes.
- Low intense walk for ten to fifteen minutes.
- Stretch for two minutes.

Wednesday

- Stretch for two minutes.
- Low intense walk for ten to fifteen minutes.
- Stretch for two minutes.
- Brisk walk for five to ten minutes.

Thursday

- Stretch for two minutes.
- Low intense walk for ten to fifteen minutes.
- Stretch for two minutes.

Friday

- Rest day! It is good to do stretches on your rest day.

Weekend

- Optional.
- Stretch for two minutes.
- Low intense walk for ten to fifteen minutes.
- Stretch for two minutes.

Week 3

Now you're ready to start week 3 of your walking exercise. For this week, we'll be leveling up the intensity even more, by introducing brisker walks into your schedule. A brisk walk means that you speed walk or walk at the fastest pace that's suitable for you. Here's a guide for your third week of walking.

Monday

- Stretch for two minutes.
- Low intense walk for ten to fifteen minutes.
- Stretch for two minutes.
- Low intense walk for ten to fifteen minutes.

Tuesday

- Stretch for two minutes.
- Low intense walk for ten to fifteen minutes.
- Stretch for two minutes.

Wednesday

- Stretch for two minutes.
- Low intense walk for ten to fifteen minutes.
- Stretch for two minutes.
- Brisk walk for 5-20 minutes

Thursday

- Stretch for two minutes.
- Low intense walk for ten to fifteen minutes.
- Stretch for two minutes.

Friday

- Rest Day! It is good to do stretches on your rest day.

Weekend

- Stretch for two minutes.
- Low intense walk for ten to fifteen minutes.
- Stretch for two minutes.
- Window shopping and keep moving!

Week 4

After three weeks of consistent walking, you should be noticing an improvement in your health and overall fitness. You're able to walk faster and for longer, so week four will push you a little harder to increase intensity and duration of your walks. Here's how you can do it.

Monday

- Stretch for two minutes.
- Low intense walk for ten to fifteen minutes.
- Stretch for two minutes.
- Brisk walk for five to ten minutes.

Tuesday

- Stretch for two minutes.
- Low intense walk for fifteen to twenty minutes.
- Stretch for two minutes.

Wednesday

- Stretch for two minutes.
- Low intense walk for ten to fifteen minutes.
- Brisk walk for five to ten minutes.
- Stretch for two minutes.

Thursday

- Stretch for two minutes.
- Low intense walk for ten to fifteen minutes.
- Stretch for two minutes.
- Brisk walk for twenty to twenty-five minutes.
- Stretch for three minutes.

Friday

- Rest day! It is good to do stretches on your rest day.

Weekend

- Stretch for two minutes.
- Low intense walk for ten to fifteen minutes.
- Stretch for two minutes.

Week 5

We're getting toward the end of the six-week beginner's walking program. Remember throughout this program, you must take the necessary rest that your body needs. However, for this week you should try to push yourself by not taking a rest day. This is how you can plan your week.

Monday

- Stretch for two minutes.
- Low intense walk for ten to fifteen minutes.
- Brisk walk for ten to fifteen minutes.
- Stretch for two minutes.

Tuesday

- Stretch for two minutes.
- Low intense walk for 25 - 30 minutes.
- Stretch for two minutes.

Wednesday

- Stretch for two minutes.
- Low intense walk for ten to fifteen minutes.
- Brisk walk for ten to fifteen minutes.
- Stretch for three minutes.

Thursday

- Stretch for two minutes.
- Low intense walk for 25 - 30 minutes.
- Stretch for three minutes.

Friday

- Alternative activity you enjoy, for example go for a swim, dancing class, or do a gardening activity.

Weekend

- Stretch for two minutes.
- Low intense walk for 25 - 30 minutes.
- Stretch for two minutes.

Week 6

For the final week of this program, you will have to push yourself. It's a bit different to the other weeks because you'll be getting into more intensive and effective ways for you to exercise your body through walking. This is how you can end your last week of your plan.

Monday

- Stretch for two minutes.
- Low intense walk for 15-20 minutes.
- Power walk for 30 seconds, Low intense walk for one minute—repeat this process four to six times.
- Low intense walk for three to five minutes.
- Stretch for two minutes.

Tuesday

- Stretch for two minutes.
- Alternative activity, cardio. Swim. Pickleball. Or whatever gets your blood pumping. 20-30 minutes.
- Stretch for two minutes.

Wednesday

- Stretch for two minutes.
- Low intense walk for 30-35 minutes.
- Stretch for four minutes.

Thursday

- Stretch for two minutes.
- Low intense walk for 25-30 minutes.
- Stretch for three minutes.

Friday

- Rest day! But do stretches on this day to stay limber.

Weekend

- Stretch for two minutes.
- Brisk walk for 25-35 minutes.
- Stretch for two minutes.

Although you may be done with this six week walking program, it doesn't mean you should end this exercise plan. It's valuable for you to make similar walking schedules for yourself every week. Making walking as a regular habit of exercise will provide you with countless benefits.

8

CORE STRENGTH

"Go the extra mile. It's never crowded."

— WAYNE DYER

Your core plays a special role in your strength and stability. If you want to prevent yourself from experiencing falls, it's important for you to strengthen your core. A strong and limber core will help you to remain stabilized when you walk and stand. Once you work on improving your overall mobility, you can do core strength exercises. They may be a bit more strenuous and intense than the other exercises, but they're still manageable and safe!

THE ROLE OF CORE STRENGTH IN FALL PREVENTION

When you think of what makes you at risk of falling more frequently, you may blame your balance, your legs, your center of gravity, and your ability to hold yourself up with your arms. Although these are all factors that contribute to your fall risk, you may be forgetting a crucial part of your falling issue—your core. Your core plays a massive role in being able to keep yourself up and sturdy. Afterall, your legs, arms and head all connect to your core. Here is the role core strength plays in falling prevention:

- **Creates stability.** The most important reason why your core should be strengthened is because it helps you to create stability. Your core is the center of your body, so it helps the other muscles in your body. If you lose your balance suddenly, your core can help you to stay stable, which ultimately prevents you from falling.
- **Developing a center of gravity.** As your body gets older, you may find that you fall over more easily. This can be due to not having a strong sense of gravity that keeps you stable. Your core acts as your center of gravity as it keeps you firm in your stance.
- **Helps you fulfill daily tasks.** Your core muscles play a role in the small tasks we accomplish during the day, for example, standing up, bending over to garden, working in the kitchen or garage, and other daily tasks. If you want to accomplish tasks with more ease, your core strength can help you with that!

When we think of exercising, we can often overlook our core muscles. We workout our arms and legs, but we ignore our core muscles. You will find that doing more core exercises completely transforms your fitness and stamina.

BENEFITS OF CORE STRENGTH

Having a strong core isn't just beneficial for your reduced fall risk, but it also provides you with other physical and health benefits. Our core can make our everyday lives so much easier and safer. If you want to make later years easier for yourself, you must prioritize your core strength.

Reduces Body Pain

If you're experiencing pain in your body, doing core exercises will help to relieve and reduce this pain. As a senior, you may experience more aches and pains, especially in your back from bad posture. When you experience your core these aches and pains in your back will diminish as you build the muscles and tendons. You will find a lot of value in core exercises.

Another way core exercises can help you is by preventing injuries and pain in the future. When you do core exercises, you reduce your risk of hurting your joints, muscles, and bones. This will prevent you from getting hurt when you exercise or when you're fulfilling daily tasks. Doing stretches that include your core will also keep your core limber.

Improves Your Posture

Often as one gets older their posture becomes bad as they are always leaning forward. This is due to not enough strength in their core to support their upper body. Causing one to slouch. This doesn't only give you back pain, but it also makes it challenging for you to move around effectively. You may struggle to walk around, fulfill daily tasks, or just feel comfortable.

When you practice core exercises frequently, you will find that your posture improves drastically. Your core helps you to stay upright, with your spine lengthened and your pelvis in natural alignment. This can help you to relieve a lot of discomfort you may be experiencing. And help prevent future discomfort.

Improves Lifting Ability

As one approaches their later years, they may find that they struggle lifting objects, especially when those objects are on the heavier side. Having a strong core can help you to lift heavy items without putting a strain on your body. When you lift objects, you must engage your core. This will enable you to carry things with ease without the threat of hurting yourself or throwing out your back.

INTEGRATING CORE STRENGTH IN YOUR LIFE

If you think about core exercises, you might be scared to get started because they may seem too intense. You might not feel ready to do these more intense exercises, and that's okay. There are some simple core exercises that you can practice frequently. You want to be able to prioritize the strength of your core because it will transform your life completely.

How to Integrate Core Strength in Your Life

Before we dive into the simple core exercises to practice, you should consider how you can make core strength a way of life for you. These core exercises aren't just something you should practice every now and then, as it needs to be something that is practiced on a consistent basis.

It's all about finding time to practice some effective core exercises. The examples of core exercises coming up are great beginner exercises that can be practiced at home when you're watching TV, hanging out with friends, or when you're doing other activities. They are really simple and can help you get started with your core strengthening journey.

Exercise 35: Tightrope Walk

A great exercise to improve your core strength and balance is the tightrope walker. You may find it challenging at first, as it requires you to walk in a straight line, but this will help you to drastically improve your balance over time. This is how you practice it:

1. Extend your arms out to your sides.
2. Use a scarf or an object that can help you to direct a straight line.
3. Walk along this straight line while maintaining your balance and posture.
4. When you get to the end of the short line raise your foot for a few seconds and then switch to the other foot.

5. As you take your steps ensure you're engaging your
   core muscles to maintain balance.

Ensure that you do this near a wall or sturdy object so that you
can hold yourself up if you feel like you are losing your balance.

Exercise 36: Side Bends

To engage your core muscles through simple exercise, you can
practice the side bends. This exercise will work your side
muscles. If you would like, you could practice this exercise
seated, but to challenge yourself more you should do it standing. This is how you do this exercise:

1. Stand with your feet hip-width apart.
2. Keep your hands to the side with a straight posture.

3. Engage those core muscles.
4. Start to lean to the right side, with your right hand moving down to your thigh and your left arm coming up and over your head.
5. Hold this tilt for fifteen seconds.
6. Return to your straight upright posture.
7. Then lean to the left side and hold it for another fifteen seconds.

You can practice this three times on each side. You need to ensure that your core muscles are engaged during this exercise. You must also make sure that you are leaning to the side, instead of leaning forward.

Exercise 37: Opposite Arm and Leg Raise

For this exercise, you will be on your hands and knees. This means you should either practice it on carpeted floors or get yourself a nice mat so that you're comfortable while doing this exercise. Here is how you practice it:

1. Get on all fours, with your hips aligned with your neck.
2. Lift your left leg up and extend it straight behind you.
3. Slowly lift your right arm off the floor and extend it straight in front of you.
4. Stay in this position for ten seconds and ensure your core is engaged.
5. Return to the original all fours position.
6. Lift your right leg and extend it.

7. Slowly lift your left arm off the floor and extend it straight in front of you.

8. Hold this position for ten seconds.

Doing this exercise with alternative limbs extended helps you to maintain your balance. When you practice it, make sure that you're moving your arms and legs slowly and steadily. Be in control of your movements. You can do this three times for each side.

MORE CHALLENGING CORE EXERCISES

If you've started off your journey of core exercises and you feel yourself getting stronger and more stable, then let's look into some more challenging core exercises. Once you're able to do these more intense and difficult exercises, your fitness level will be better than it's ever been.

Exercise 38: The Plank

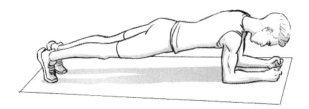

This is a very common core exercise that you have probably done before. It relies on your core strength carrying your body weight. The plank doesn't only exercise your core, as it also strengthens your arms. While doing this exercise make sure your hips aren't drooping toward the floor or hiking up toward the ceiling. You want to keep your body as straight as possible. Here's how you practice the plank safely:

1. Start with your knees on the floor.
2. Place your forearms on the floor, with your fists tightened.
3. Keep your toes planted on the ground.
4. Lift your knees off the ground and straighten your legs as much as possible.

5. Tighten your core.
6. Hold this plank position for up to 10 breaths.
7. Return to a relaxed position.
8. Do this exercise 3 times.

If you feel as though the plank is a bit challenging, you can practice a modified version of the plank. You practice it the same as the steps stated, but instead you don't lift your knees off the floor.

Exercise 39: The Bridge

For this exercise, you will not only strengthen your core muscles, as you will also be engaging your glutes. Ensure that you're doing it on a comfortable surface, like a carpet or yoga mat, because you will be doing this exercise lying on the floor. This is how to practice the bridge:

1. Lie on your back on the floor with your knees bent and your feet flat on the ground.
2. Put your arms at your sides with your palms on the floor.
3. Tighten your glutes as you lift your hips off the floor.
4. Your body should be a straight line from your hips to your shoulders.
5. Hold this position for ten seconds.
6. Return to your position on the floor.

You can repeat this exercise ten times. Each time you must ensure that not only your glutes are engaged, but also your core muscles.

Exercise 40: The Superman

This exercise is done on the floor, but you'll be doing it lying on your stomach. This exercise will target your core, back muscles, and your glutes. Here's how to practice it:

1. Lie on my stomach.
2. Reach your arms out above your head, so your body is in a straight line.
3. Lift your head, right arm, and left leg at the same time off the ground.
4. Return to your starting position.
5. Alternate to your other side by lifting your head, left arm, and right leg.
6. Keep on alternating until you do this 10 times for each side.

As you do this, you should be feeling it in your glutes, core, and back muscles. Ensure that you're practicing it slow and steady so that you don't pull anything.

Exercise 41: The Dead Bug

This exercise is extremely effective at strengthening your abdominal muscles. This is how you practice the dead bug:

1. Lie on your back with your legs lifted and your knees bent. Like if you were sitting in a chair but laying on your back. Both your arms will be extended out in front of you over your chest. This is the starting position.
2. Straighten out your right leg toward the floor, while you extend your left arm over your head and towards the floor.

3. Return to the starting position.
4. Straighten out your left leg toward the floor, while you extend your right arm over your head and towards the floor.
5. Return to the starting position.
6. Continue alternating this until you do it 20 times.

While doing the Dead Bug exercise keep your back flat on the ground and take your movements nice and slow. You can start off by doing the Dead Bug 5 times and then move up you 10 when 5 is easy to do. The idea is to work up to doing it 20 times.

CREATE CORE EXERCISE ROUTINE

If you want to ensure that your core gets strong, you need to be able to practice these exercises frequently. Try out all the exercises throughout this chapter, starting off with beginner's level and working your way up to more challenging exercises.

Once you find the exercises that you enjoy the most, you can create a core exercise routine that you can add to your exercise routine. Doing these exercises on a daily basis will help your balance and strength, as well as improve your performance with all your other exercises.

9

IMPROVING YOUR BALANCING ABILITY

"We do not stop exercising because we grow old- we grow old because we stop exercising"

— DR. KENNETH COOPER

Some of us struggle to balance, especially when we're over the age of 60. If balancing is something you really struggle with, there are balancing activities that will help to balance a lot better. These exercises will help prevent you from falling as easily.

HOW TO IMPROVE YOUR BALANCING

Ultimately, your goal for exercising is to strengthen yourself and your balance so you can have a great standard of living in your later years. Part of that would be having less aches and pains and not becoming a victim to a bad fall impairing your enjoyment of life. If you find your balancing issues are holding you back from progressing with your exercise, specific exercises can be done to improve this.

These exercises are geared towards improving your balance.

Take Precautions

Before we dive into the different balance exercises you can do, it's important for you to be cautious when exercising. If balancing is something you struggle with because of medication, health conditions, joint pain, or other issues, you need to make sure you practice activities safely. These are some crucial precautions you should consider if you struggle with balancing:

- **Use a stable surface.** The environment you choose to do these exercises is crucial. You need to be able to choose a location that is safe and suitable for your standing and seated exercises. Ensure that you're exercising on a level floor that doesn't have any holes or declines, as well as avoid any type of slippery floors. Doing this will prevent any unnecessary falls or slips that compromise your balance. This would also extends out to exercising where that aren't random objects that could become a trip hazards.
- **Sit or lie down when you need to.** If you feel that all of a sudden your balance is compromised, you should sit down immediately. You may find yourself feeling dizzy or light-headed, so it's important to stop yourself then and there so you avoid a fall. If you're not feeling well

while exercising, you must take a break to regather yourself.

- **Have something to hold on to.** If you are at a high falling risk because of a lack of balance, you should always exercise with something to hold onto. You can have a chair close by that can provide support whenever you feel as though you're out of balance. You can also use this chair to sit down during the intervals of your exercise, to ensure that you're healthy and physically stable.
- **Let others know you are exercising.** When you are engaging on your exercise journey, let others know when and where you will be exercising. This can be family and friends that are close by. That way they can check in on you and help you if needed.

If you ensure all of these precautions are put in place, you shouldn't be worrying about falling when you exercise. Try to embrace each activity to the fullest. You need to be able to trust yourself or else you won't be able to get all the benefits from your exercising journey. This is why it may be effective for you to practice some balancing exercises, to ensure that you maintain a healthy balance through all your physical activities.

Exercise, Exercise, Exercise!

As you probably know by now, the main way for you to improve your balancing is through exercising. Although there may be some other factors that contribute to your balancing problems, exercise will be the best solution to get you on track with balancing. Unfortunately, for many of us, being able to stick to exercising can be really challenging. This is how you can make the most out of your exercising so that it optimizes your balancing skills:

- **Practice those balancing exercises.** You may be focusing on exercise because you want to get stronger and fitter, which can often make you overlook the balancing exercises. If you want to improve your ability of balancing, you need to be able to add these balancing activities to your exercise routines. Doing this before your other exercises will help you to have a more stable and productive workout.
- **Challenge your balance with each exercise.** If you want to be an overachiever, by getting yourself to balance under more intense scenarios, you can find ways to challenge your balance through everyday activities. When you're doing a standing exercise, you can challenge your balance by standing on one leg. Doing small things like this during your workouts will not only improve your balance, but it will also push your muscles.
- **Make time to practice balancing.** This is all about finding the time to make practicing balancing a way of life. You can take any opportunity, like during your exercises, when you're walking around, or when you're fulfilling daily tasks. You'd be surprised to discover the opportunities throughout the day you have to challenge and improve your balancing abilities.

The more you practice your balancing skills, the more stable you will feel. Although most balancing activities are low intensive and may not build muscles the way you'd like, they will build your skill and confidence. When you feel stable and balanced it makes you feel more confident in yourself, which can also make you feel more confident in your exercises and boing about your business on a daily basis.

Consider What Makes You Unbalanced

If you find yourself still struggling with your balance even though you're exercising frequently, you may want to pursue other factors and issues that are negatively impacting your balancing skills. If you are really struggling with your balance, these are some things you should consider so that you can get to the root of the issue:

- **Medication.** One of the main factors that could be contributing to your balancing issues is the medication you may be taking. If you have a medical condition, you could take a wide variety of medications that make you feel light-headed and dizzy. If this is a factor you think may be contributing to your balancing issues, you should visit the doctor for a solution. Let him know what is occurring and what solutions there are for this.
- **Hazardous environment.** Maybe the problem isn't that you're unbalanced, but it's your environment. If you are in a house with slippery floors and tiles, you may find yourself out of balance easily. If your home is filled with clutter and objects lying around, you may trip and lose

your balance. Sometimes your issue may not be your balance, but it's your environment that causes you to trip and fall.

- **Head injury.** If you've fallen down recently and hurt your head, this can have a massive impact on your balance. If you have experienced a bad fall and your head was hit on impact, you need to visit a doctor immediately. This fall could've had a greater impact on you, which causes you to feel dizzy and unbalanced. Ultimately, this can cause you to lose your balance and fall again.
- **Ear infection.** A major cause of dizziness and feeling unbalanced is when you have an ear infection. Having an ear infection or an issue with your ears can make you topple over. If you feel ear pain and uncontrollable dizziness, you should go to the doctor to check it out.
- **Low blood pressure.** Another common factor that could make you feel unbalanced is having low blood pressure. If you stand up quickly, you may feel light-headed and unbalanced. If you have low blood pressure, you must visit your doctor and ask for solutions that can help you to improve your balance.

You should consider all of these factors if you're really struggling with your balance. You may have a health related issue that causes you to lose your balance. If you think there's a deeper reason, go and visit your doctor so you can get to the bottom of this issue. Then you can practice the following balancing exercises to further improve your balance.

BALANCING EXERCISES

If your balance is something that's really holding you back when you're doing these exercises, these are just a few separate balancing activities that you may want to add to your exercise. Balancing is crucial for you along this journey and in life. You should incorporate some of these balancing exercises daily.

Exercise 42: Rock The Boat

This is a great balancing exercise for you to try out, as it's simple and effective. Being able to stand firmly while doing an exercise on one foot can be challenging, but practicing an activity like this frequently will help you to be more balanced in your everyday life. Follow these steps:

1. Stand with your feet hip-width apart.
2. Stand up straight with a leveled head.
3. Slowly lift your left leg, as you lean all of your weight onto your right foot.
4. You can then slowly shift to the other side.
5. You can rock back and forth, swapping the weight from your left and right side around 15-20 times.

If you struggle to balance while doing this exercise, the use a chair or sturdy object to help you keep your balance is advised.

Exercise 43: Flamingo Stand

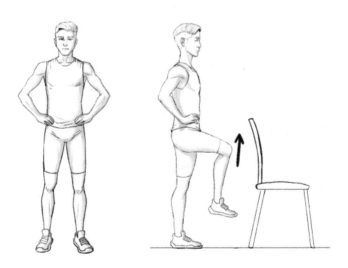

This standing exercise can help you to train your body to be more balanced as you stand. For this exercise, you should get a chair or wall to lean on, as you'll be balancing on one leg. This is how you go about practicing the Flamingo Stand:

1. Stand with your legs hip-width apart.
2. Place your hands on your hips.
3. Keep your back upright and straight.
4. Lift your right leg, bending your knee. If you lose balance hold onto the wall or chair for support while you regain your balance.
5. Hold this position for fifteen seconds.
6. Do the same activity for your left leg.

If you're feeling brave and you want to increase the intensity of this exercise, you can get your arms involved. As you lift your right leg, you can extend your right arm to reach for it, and the same goes with your left arm and left leg. Only do this if you're feeling confident in your balance.

Exercise 44: Single Leg Stance

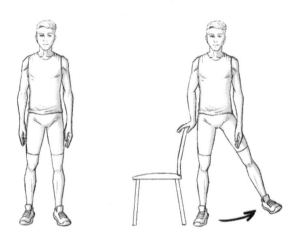

For this activity, you must ensure you're with someone else or next to a chair so that you don't put yourself in any danger. As with the other exercises, you will be standing on one leg. Here is how you can practice this single legged balancing activity:

1. Ensure your feet are flat and sturdy, placed directly under your hips.
2. Slowly swing your left leg out to the side.
3. Hold onto something if you feel yourself losing balance.
4. Hold this position for fifteen seconds.
5. Bring your left leg back to the starting position.
6. Practice the same motion with your right leg.

Many of the other exercises in this book will help you to work on your balance, especially the exercises that are practiced standing. Consider any of these exercises that challenge your balancing skills, as you can add them to your exercise routine.

VESTIBULAR EXERCISES

If you are out of balance because of medical conditions, ear infections, or your eyesight, it's valuable for you to do some vestibular exercises. Vestibular activities train your brain to comprehend dizziness and balance. For these exercises, you must work on your eyesight and head movements. You must practice head movements that cause dizziness, as well as spontaneous movements that would cause you to lose your balance. The following exercises should be done standing but can also be done sitting down or holding onto a chair, wall or stable object. This would be a gradient to doing the exercises standing.

Exercise 45: Eye Stabilization

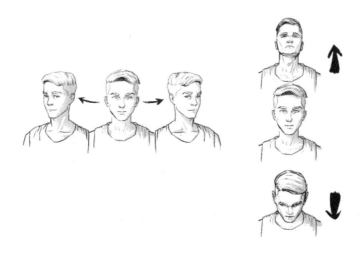

When you consider balancing exercises, you must also consider working your eyes. We can often forget that our eyes play a massive role in our ability to find stability and balance. You want to train your eyes to move independently from your head. For this eye stabilization exercise, you will train your eyes and mind to focus on an object, even if you're moving. Here's how to practice it:

1. Find a stationary object to focus on.
2. Keep your eyes focused on it and step several feet away from it.
3. Ensure your eye remains on the target as you move your head to the right.
4. Keep focused as you then move your head to the left.

5. Maintain focus as you slowly move your head up and down.

If you're able to do this without losing eye contact with the object, it's a good sign. You should practice this exercise 5 times on different objects. If you find yourself feeling dizzy from the head movements, you can sit down and practice. As you get better at this exercise, you should make it more challenging. You can choose smaller objects, step further away, and move your head faster and further.

Exercise 46: Head Rotation

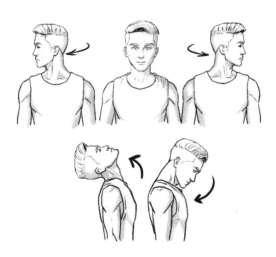

To introduce your body to head movements that cause dizziness, you should try out some head rotation exercises. You can practice this exercise seated, but if you want to get your body used to dizziness, you may want to try this head rotation standing up. This is how you can practice it:

1. Straighten your posture.
2. Slowly turn your head to the right.
3. Bring your head back to the center, then turn your head to the left.
4. Practice this five times.
5. Then center your head and start looking up slowly and then down.
6. Do this five times.

When you do the Head Rotation exercise, you may experience some dizziness. Do this slowly and steadily and keep on doing it. It will help with your perception of balance when you may need it the most.

CREATING BALANCING EXERCISING ROUTINE

You want to be able to put as much attention on your balancing as you would for all of your other exercises. It can be easy to neglect your balance exercises, because they may not feel like a proper workout like your other exercises. This is how you can add balancing exercises to your routine in the most effective way possible:

- **Add three balancing activities.** You don't have to add all of these exercises into your schedule. All you need are three effective balancing exercises that target exactly what you need. You should try out all the balancing activities to determine which three are best for you. They must all do various movements so that you introduce a diversity into your exercise routine. These can also be switched out in the future for other balance exercises to address other balancing scenarios.

- **Persevere through the dizziness.** When you're getting started with balancing exercises, you must be prepared to experience discomfort. At first you will probably feel dizzy, but this is something you must push through. You may find that you're even dizzier than usual, which may make you want to give up. Instead of feeling discouraged, persevere through the dizziness, just ensure you have the necessary precautions to keep you safe.
- **Practice them for one or two minutes.** If you want to make the most of these balancing exercises, you mustn't just do it once and get it over with. You need to be able to practice these exercises long enough for it to be truly beneficial and effective. When you start off, you should do each exercise for one minute, but as you progress and get fitter, you should push yourself by doing each exercise for more than 2 minutes.

Once these balancing exercises become a way of life for you, your risk of falling will decrease dramatically. Being able to keep your stability will help you to go about daily activities and your exercises without putting yourself in harm's way.

STRETCH FOR SUCCESS

"Even if you don't have time for a big workout, stretching in the morning and night really changes your body."

— ERIN HEATHERTON

With any form of exercise that you embrace, you need to be sure to do the necessary stretches before and after. Stretching will help you to become more flexible and it will prepare your muscles before you exercise, as well as it will soothe your muscles after you practice exercises. If you don't stretch properly, you could pull a muscle or tendon and no one what's that.

THE IMPORTANCE OF STRETCHING

One of the most important components of successful exercise is being able to do your stretches. Stretching is important for any individual to do when exercising, but it's even more important for seniors. As your body ages and your muscle mass decreases, the body tends to get stiff and not as limber as it once was. If you want to have a safe and successful exercise session, it's valuable to prioritize your stretches!

Promotes Flexibility

The main reason why stretching is so important for you when you're exercising is because it promotes flexibility. You may find that as you get older your muscles and joints become a lot stiffer. You aren't able to move the way you used to because of this stiffness.

For many of the exercises in this book, you will need to practice more flexibility than you may be used to. It isn't intense flexibility, but it may be more than you'd practice in your everyday life. Bending and manipulating your body in different positions is a great and effective way to exercise your muscles. If you aren't flexible for some exercises, you might end up pulling something and getting hurt.

Dangers of Neglecting Stretching

As we've established, stretching is crucial for any person exercising, but it's even more important for seniors. When you don't do stretches as an older person, you may find that it actually endangers you. You need to be able to stretch every time you work out both before and after so that you don't put yourself in harm's way. These are just a few dangers you could experience from neglecting your stretching:

- **Feeling sick.** Not stretching when you exercise can actually make you feel sick during your workout. You just jump into your exercise, and this ends up shocking your system. You may find that you get light-headed, as your body wasn't prepared for the blood flow. You may also feel nauseous and weak.
- **Your muscles will feel stiff and sore.** When you push yourself with exercise, your muscles need to be stretched. If you do a lot of intensive exercise one day and leave it at that without stretching, the next day you will feel the pain in your muscles. You may struggle to bend, move around, and fulfill daily tasks because of this muscle pain and stiffness.
- **You are at risk of injury.** Ironically, if you exercise without stretching you may end up injuring yourself, which is the whole reason why you may be exercising in the first place. You're trying to get stronger to prevent falls and injury in your future, so you don't want to end up hurting yourself through exercise because you're not stretching enough.

Ultimately, stretching is what will keep you on track with your fitness journey!

DIFFERENT KINDS OF STRETCHES

Before we go into detail about the different stretches you could do for your various body parts, it's important to know the kinds of stretches out there. There are different kinds of stretches that can provide you with their own benefits. Knowing the different types of stretches can help you find what's best for you and your body:

- **Ballistic stretching.** Ballistic means: Moving under the force of gravity. Ballistic stretching is a type of stretch that involves gravity and bouncing or swinging motions. To perform this stretching, you use the momentum of your body to force stretches at a fast speed. For example, you may swing your leg back and forth quickly to stretch your leg muscles.
- **Dynamic stretching.** Dynamic stretches are a form of stretches where muscles and joints go through a full range of motion. Dynamic stretches are done at a controlled speed, as well as you increase the intensity of your stretches as you see fit. This is a more suitable form of stretching for your muscles, as you are controlling how you move your muscles and how much you stretch them.
- **Active stretching.** Active stretching is when you get into a muscle activating position and you hold it. You activate your muscles to keep you in this stretching position. For example, you may lift your leg up until your knee reaches hip level. You have to engage your core and leg muscles to keep you stable in this position.

- **Passive stretching.** Passive stretches are similar to active stretches as you get into a position and hold it, but instead of engaging specific muscles to stay in this position, you use an object or person to keep you in this pose. You may even use your hand to hold your body in this position.

When people think of stretching, they may have a one-sided idea of how to do it. You may think that you're doing stretching in the most effective manner by simply moving your body around, but you may find that your technique is more unhelpful than you may think. Your stretching may do the opposite of what it's intended for by causing you to injure yourself.

STRETCHING BEFORE EXERCISE

Before you even think about getting started with your exercises for the day, you must start off with some stretches. Stretching before your exercises will loosen up your muscles and tendons, which will help your performance during your exercise. Stretching will get your blood flowing, which gives you more energy and ability to dive into your exercises.

Another reason why stretching is so crucial is that it warms your muscles up. This is especially important if you haven't exercised in a long time. You can't just jump into an exercise and expect to be fine. You need to warm up these muscles with the right stretches. This will allow your muscles to be prepared for any exercises coming its way.

You will find that with stretches, you're able to do a larger range of motions, as your muscles are more flexible and ready. You will also be able to do more exercises, as your muscles feel more durable and energized. Your exercise will be all round more beneficial, as your muscles are able to perform specific and better movements.

STRETCHING AFTER EXERCISE

Many people think about stretching before their exercise, but they neglect it afterward. If you don't want to feel sore the next day or feel experience fatigue and struggle when you try to exercise again, you must stretch after your exercises.

When you stretch after an exercise, it prevents you from being sore the next day. It also avoids your muscles from feeling overly fatigued. When you stretch your muscles, you reduce the amount of lactic acid (an acid your body produces in the muscle tissue during strenuous exercise) throughout your body. When you work out, you produce a lot of lactic acid, which could make your muscles ache and feel tired. This will negatively impact your performance the next day. Stretching is the best way for you to eliminate excess lactic acid in your body. Also doing a "cool down" walk will help run out any excess lactic acid in your system.

After an exercise, your body is bound to feel a bit tense and stiff, especially if you worked out hard and challenged yourself. This makes stretching after your exercise imperative, as it will loosen those tense and stiff muscles. Your body becomes more relaxed, which can help you wind-down for the day.

Stretching after an exercise is not only valuable for you physically, as it can also benefit you mentally. When you're exercising and pushing yourself, you may get into a serious mental state to keep yourself going. You need to transition from this energetic and intense mental state, to a more relaxed and calmer one. This can help you to have a peaceful and enjoyable day further.

STRETCHES FOR SUCCESS

Now that you know the importance of stretching both before and after your exercises, it's valuable to get into some stretches you can practice. These stretches will make up your exercises in this book. We will cover a stretch you can do for each part of your body. Ensure that you find a stretching routine that's effective for you that targets all of your muscles!

Exercise 47: Feet Stretch

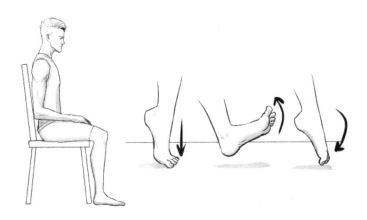

When you think of stretching for your exercise, you may not see relevance or value in stretching your feet. We can often forget about this side of our body, but stretching our feet can help us to perform exercises more effectively. You want to ensure that your feet are in good shape so that you don't hurt them during your workout or in your everyday life. This is a simple foot stretch that will get this part of your body warmed up or cooled down:

1. Sit down with your feet flat on the ground.
2. Keep your toes planted on the ground as you lift your heels.
3. Hold this for five seconds and then lower your heels back to the ground.

4. Raise your toes, with your heels planted on the ground.
5. Hold this for five seconds then lower your toes.
6. Curl your toes and raise your heels.
7. Hold this for five seconds and then lower.
8. Run through this stretch 3 times.

Doing this activity will help you exercise your whole foot, especially your toes. The grip strength in your feet can help you to walk and exercise.

Exercise 48: Hand Stretch

We've done a few hand stretching exercises earlier on in this book that are all valuable exercises that will get those hands warmed up. Stretching your hands won't only help you with your exercises, but it will also improve your grip strength. You may find that as you get older, you struggle to grab and hold onto things like you used to. Try the hand strengthening exercises, and this wrist stretching exercise:

1. Put your hands together in a prayer position in front of your mouth.
2. Separate your elbows and lower your hands in the prayer position, until your hands reach your belly button.
3. Hold this stretch for 20 seconds.
4. Repeat this two times.

When you have both better grip strength and wrist mobility, you will find it a lot easier to fulfill daily tasks.

Exercise 49: Leg Stretch

Every person should be doing leg stretches when they do workouts, go for a walk, or participate in any other form of physical activity. However, it's especially important for you to do leg stretches as a senior. By not being as active as you once were one tends to do a lot of sitting. This can make your leg muscles weaker and less used to physical activity, so you need to do stretches to warm them up. Here's how you go about doing a leg stretch:

1. Start by standing with your legs hip-width apart.
2. Slightly bend your knees and keep your hands by your sides.
3. Inhale deeply and lift your arms above your head.
4. As you exhale, roll your upper body forward.

5. Keep your head, neck, and shoulders relaxed as you bend your torso as far down as possible.
6. You should be feeling a stretch in your hamstrings, the back of your legs.
7. Hold this position for 30 seconds.
8. When you're coming up, bend your knees.

Practice this exercise three times to feel a great stretch. Ensure that you get up slowly and steadily after each stretch. If you get up too quickly, you may find yourself feeling dizzy.

Exercise 50: Arm Stretches

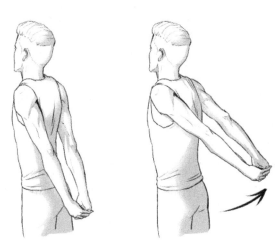

If you are a stronger individual with muscles in your arms, you may think you don't require arm stretches, but this couldn't be further from the truth. No matter how weak or strong your arms are, you need to stretch them before you exercise them. Here is an arm stretching exercise to try out:

1. Reach your arms behind your back, bringing your palms together so your hands grip each other.
2. As you breathe in, bring your hands outward and upwards.
3. You will feel a stretch in your arms, shoulders, and chest.
4. Hold this for ten seconds.
5. Rotate your hands to face downward once again.
6. Separate your hands and bring them to your side.

This stretch is similar to the hand stretch we discussed earlier, but instead of doing it in front of you, you do it behind your back. This gives your arms a full stretch. It targets both your forearms and your shoulders.

Exercise 51: Hip Stretch

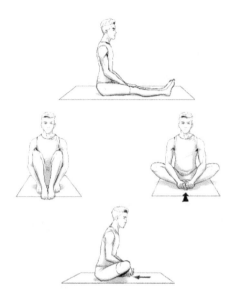

It's very common to have issues with one's hips as a senior. This makes it valuable for you to practice hip stretches to ease the pain and open up this area. You will find that hip stretches help you to perform your exercises better. This is a great hip stretching activity to do:

1. Sit on the floor, with a straight posture.
2. Place the soles of your feet together while bending your knees.
3. Bring your feet as close to your pelvis as possible.
4. It may be challenging for you to hold this position, so you should hold your ankles or feet.
5. Press your knees outward and toward the floor.
6. Hold this for 30 seconds.

7. For an extra challenge, you can bend your torso forward with your legs in this position.
8. Do this stretch 2 – 3 times.

For this exercise, you will not only open your hips, but you will also stretch your glutes and thighs. This will help you to do any exercises that engage your leg muscles.

Exercise 52: Lower Back Stretch

Another common pain one may get in their later years is lower back pain. It can be easy to injure your back, so stretching it regularly will not only help you to reduce lower back pain, but it will also help prevent you from pulling a muscle or tendon in the future. Here is a stretching exercise that will relieve pain in your lower back:

1. Lie down on your back with your legs extended and your arms by your side.
2. Pull your left knee up to your chest, while your right leg remains straightly extended.
3. Keep your lower back pressed down toward the floor.
4. Hold this position for 30 seconds to a minute.
5. Repeat this stretch with your right leg.
6. Repeat this stretch 3 – 5 times on each side.

When you do this stretch, you will be able to relieve any pain you're experiencing in your lower back. It will also stretch the muscles and joints in your lower back, which will prevent you from potentially pulling your lower back out. This stretch will also stretch your hamstrings and open your hips up.

EVENING WIND-DOWN STRETCHES

If stretching isn't something you have the time or energy to do at the moment, having an evening wind-down stretching session every night will help you overcome that. And the stretches themselves will help you immensely. It's as simple as setting aside 10 minutes to get some quality stretches in. Just lake forming any habit, one needs to set the time and location the stretches will be performed.

This will ensure that you stretch out the muscles you worked on so that they aren't painful when you wake up the next morning. You may also find that doing stretches every night helps to strengthen your muscles in many ways. Even if you don't exercise that day, you can benefit from some evening stretches.

CONCLUSION

"Motivation is what gets you started. Habit is what keeps you going."

— JIM RYUN

Getting old shouldn't be something to fear and stress over. It's a way of life and whether we like it or not, we're all going to approach this stage of our lives. Instead of fearing it and the safety threats and risks that may come with older age, it's time for you to embrace it so you can make the most of your life.

You don't want a big fall to be the reason why your quality of life diminishes drastically, because you still have so much life to live. This is why it's crucial to work toward reducing your risk of falling. When you work on your physical and mental fitness through effective and consistent exercise, your likelihood of falling will decrease dramatically. This will ultimately allow you to experience your later years in peace and happiness.

When we're younger, we take our health and fitness for granted. This can cause us to have unhealthy habits that negatively impact us when we age. You may find that this habitual behavior catches up with you in your old age, as you start to age rapidly physically. You may experience health conditions, body pains, or physical and mental deterioration.

Taking your health and fitness seriously now is the best way to reclaim your youth. Motivation will get you started, but habit will keep you going. When you start this fitness journey and you're consistent, set up daily exercise habits that you can follow, and you will feel less limited by your age. Your risk of falling will decline dramatically, as your body gets stronger and more balanced.

Joe's success story should motivate you to keep on working toward your fitness. His mobility was stunted, as he used a wheelchair. Through his challenging but successful fitness journey, he got out of the wheelchair, and now he uses a walker. He accomplished his goal of being able to walk again, as it gave him a sense of pride and independence.

Joe had a can-do attitude and a willingness to try, which pushed him through his fitness journey. The support and love from his family also gave him the inspiration to improve his mobility. You can use this story as motivation to push you through your fitness journey. Although it may not be easy, it will be worth it.

You too can achieve amazing results through your fitness journey. You don't have to be a victim to the aches and pains, which prevent you from enjoying your everyday life. You can do the activities that you enjoy the most, that you may have put off because of your age and mobility. This stage of your life should not be painful and scary, so having a fear of falling and suffering as a consequence, shouldn't even be a thought you experience. Once you get fitter and healthier, the threat of falling will not stop you from living your life to the fullest.

If you enjoyed this book and learnt new exercises you can try at home, please leave a review. It's lovely to hear your feedback, as well as stories to discover how these exercises have improved your overall health and fitness and reduced your fall risk!

service@yellowworkoutbook.com

GLOSSARY

Bone density — The mass of bone mineral in your bone tissue.

Eye stabilization — Being able to keep your eyes focused on an object, regardless of your movement.

Hazardous environment — An environment with dangerous conditions that may compromise your safety.

Osteoporosis — A disease that thins the inside of your bone, decreasing your bone density.

Resorption — The absorption of your cells and tissues.

Schizoid — A condition that causes people to avoid social interactions, as they are emotionally detached from people.

Stabilization — The ability to stand sturdy without losing balance and falling.

Strength training — A variety of exercises that train resistance and improve your strength and endurance.

REFERENCES

Allen, D., Ribeiro, L., Arshad, Q., & Seemungal, B. M. (2016). *Age-related vestibular loss: Current understanding and future research directions.* Frontiers in Neurology, 7. https://doi.org/10.3389/fneur.2016.00231

American Nurse. (2015). *American Nurse today official journal of the American Nurses Association (ANA).* American Nurse. https://www.myamerican nurse.com/assessing-patients-risk-falling/

Billowits, E. (n.d.). *Success story: From wheelchair to walker. Fitness for Seniors.* Www.vintagefitness.ca. Retrieved November 21, 2022, from https://www.vintagefitness.ca/blog/2021/11/05/success-story-from-wheelchair-to-walker

Blick, K. (2017, December 14). *Combat the health risks that come with prolonged sitting by using these simple but effective seated yoga poses and stretches.* Www.allinahealth.org. https://www.allinahealth.org/healthysetgo/move/energize-your-workday-with-upperbody-chair-yoga

Brain & spine foundation | Vestibular rehabilitation exercises. (2017). Brainandspine.org.uk. https://www.brainandspine.org.uk/our-publica tions/our-fact-sheets/vestibular-rehabilitation-exercises/

Centers for Disease Control and Prevention. (2020, September 30). *Facts about falls.* Www.cdc.gov. https://www.cdc.gov/falls/facts.html

Cronkleton, E. (2018, February 15). *Yoga for neck pain: 12 Poses to try.* Healthline. https://www.healthline.com/health/yoga-for-neck-pain#poses

Cronkleton, E. (2019, February 12). *Lower back stretches: 7 Essential moves for pain relief & strength.* Healthline. https://www.healthline.com/health/lower-back-stretches

Davis, N. (2018, September 18). *How to inhale and exhale your way to better, stronger fitness.* Healthline. https://www.healthline.com/health/fitness-exercise/when-to-inhale-and-exhale-during-exercise

Flexibility training: Types of stretching. (2020, March 9). FLX. https://flxstretch training.com/blogs/news/flexibility-training-types-of-stretching

Harvard Health Publishing. (2021a, April 1). *The best core exercises for older adults.* Harvard Health. https://www.health.harvard.edu/staying-healthy/the-best-core-exercises-for-older-adults

Harvard Health Publishing. (2021b, October 13). *Strength training builds more than muscles - Harvard Health.* Harvard Health; Harvard Health. https://www.health.harvard.edu/staying-healthy/strength-training-builds-more-than-muscles

Harvard Health Publishing. (2022a, February 2). *Exercises and stretches to keep your feet healthy.* Harvard Health. https://www.health.harvard.edu/staying-healthy/exercises-and-stretches-for-foot-health

Harvard Health Publishing. (2022b, March 14). *The importance of stretching - Harvard Health.* Harvard Health; Harvard Health. https://www.health.harvard.edu/staying-healthy/the-importance-of-stretching

Healthline Editorial Team. (2014, July 14). *Stretches for wrists and hands.* Healthline; Healthline Media. https://www.healthline.com/health/chronic-pain/wrist-and-hand-stretches

Heart of Ida. (2017, September 10). *Fall Stories – Real talk from real people about falls and falls prevention – Heart of Ida.* Heart of Ida. https://www.heartofida.org/fall-stories-real-talk-from-real-people-about-falls-and-falls-prevention/

Holly, A. (2021, July 15). *The BEST 60 hard work quotes to motivate and empower you.* Quoteflick.com. https://quoteflick.com/hard-work-quotes/

How much physical activity do older adults need? (2019). Cdc.gov. https://www.cdc.gov/physicalactivity/basics/older_adults/index.htm

Kerr, C. (2021, April 25). *Top 50 motivational workout quotes.* Upper Hand. https://upperhand.com/50-motivational-workout-quotes/

Lifeline. (n.d.). *14 Exercises for seniors to improve strength and balance.* Philips Lifeline. https://www.lifeline.ca/en/resources/14-exercises-for-seniors-to-improve-strength-and-balance/

Liochev, S. (2015). *Which is the most significant cause of aging?* Antioxidants, 4(4), 793–810. https://doi.org/10.3390/antiox4040793

Marchese, G. (2021, April 10). *8 Yoga poses to soothe neck pain & tension.* Yoga Journal. https://www.yogajournal.com/poses/anatomy/neck/8-yoga-poses-to-soothe-neck-tension/

Martin, F. (2021, February 28). *Chair Yoga Precautions.* Aura Wellness Center. https://aurawellnesscenter.com/2021/02/28/chair-yoga-precautions/

Marturana, A. (2017). *The 21 best stretching exercises for better flexibility.* SELF. https://www.self.com/gallery/essential-stretches-slideshow

Medline Plus. (2021, March 30). *Fall Risk Assessment: MedlinePlus Medical Test.* Medlineplus.gov. https://medlineplus.gov/lab-tests/fall-risk-assessment/

Mortimer, J. (n.d.). *John Mortimer Quotes.* BrainyQuote. Retrieved November 18, 2022, from https://www.brainyquote.com/quotes/john_mor timer_986235?src=t_aging

NHS. (2020, April 30). *Warm-up and cool-down.* Www.nhsinform.scot. https:// www.nhsinform.scot/healthy-living/keeping-active/before-and-after-exercise/warm-up-and-cool-down

Pelzer, K. (2021, September 24). *Take a deep breath in, now release, and find inner peace with these 100 Yoga Quotes!* Parade: Entertainment, Recipes, Health, Life, Holidays. https://parade.com/1158471/kelseypelzer/yoga-quotes/

Pizer, A. (2022, November 4). *10 Yoga poses you can do in a chair.* Verywell Fit. https://www.verywellfit.com/chair-yoga-poses-3567189

Positivity, P. of. (2020, June 8). *Yogi reveals 10 chair yoga moves for people with knee pain.* Power of Positivity: Positive Thinking & Attitude. https://www. powerofpositivity.com/chair-yoga-seated-poses-for-knee-pain/

Publishing, H. H. (2015, July 15). *Ask the doctor: Stretching before exercise.* Harvard Health. https://www.health.harvard.edu/staying-healthy/ask-the-doctor-stretching-before-exercise

Reinburg, S. (n.d.). *Falls are increasingly lethal for older Americans.* WebMD. https://www.webmd.com/healthy-aging/news/20190604/study-older-americans-are-dying-more-from-falls

Ribaudo, A., & Alva, S. (2021, January 19). *10 Stretches to do before bed to improve your sleep.* Hospital for Special Surgery. https://www.hss.edu/arti cle_stretches-before-bed.asp

Schlinger, A. (2020, May 15). *The best walking workout for older people.* Healthy. https://www.thehealthy.com/exercise/walking/walking-workout-older-people/

Simon, S. (2019, October 23). *5 Benefits of strength training.* Www.cancer.org. https://www.cancer.org/latest-news/five-benefits-of-strength-training.html

Snug Safety. (2020, June 5). *5 Core exercises for seniors: Build strength from your center.* Snug Safety. https://www.snugsafe.com/all-posts/core-exercises-for-seniors

Star, K. (2019). *Visualization techniques can help manage your symptoms.* Verywell Mind. https://www.verywellmind.com/visualization-for-relaxation-2584112

Stelter, G. (2016, May 12). *Arm stretches: For flexibility.* Healthline. https:// www.healthline.com/health/fitness-exercise/arm-stretches

Theifels, J. (2017, April 21). *How to breathe while working out, exercising.* AARP. https://www.aarp.org/health/healthy-living/info-2017/breathe-exercise-workout.html

UCI Health. (2018, March 15). *Oh, my aging eyes! What can I do to preserve sight?* Www.ucihealth.org. https://www.ucihealth.org/blog/2018/03/aging-eye

UMMC Health Care. (n.d.). *Vestibular exercises.* University of Mississippi Medical Center. https://www.umc.edu/Healthcare/ENT/Patient-Handouts/Adult/Otology/Vestibular_Exercises.html

Watson, K. (2019, July 23). *6 Simple, effective stretches to do after your workout.* Healthline; Healthline Media. https://www.healthline.com/health/fitness-exercise/stretching-after-workout

Wetherell, J. (2020). *I'm very anxious about falling. What can I do? | Anxiety and Depression Association of America, ADAA.* Adaa.org. https://adaa.org/living-with-anxiety/older-adults/fear-of-falling

Winder, A. M. (2022, May 14). *12 Hip stretches your body really needs.* SELF. https://www.self.com/gallery/hip-stretches-your-body-really-needs-slideshow

Top 50 Motivational Workout Quotes - Upper Hand

76 Funny Quotes About Getting Older To Bring You Laughter (quote-flick.com)

Made in the USA
Las Vegas, NV
03 December 2024

13183119R00108